THE 12 STEPS

TO BOUNDARYLESS SUCCESS

Your Time Is Now

BRETT K. OUBRE

THE 12 STEPS

TO BOUNDARYLESS SUCCESS

ISBN 979-8-9860859-9-9

PUBLISHED IN THE UNITED STATES OF AMERICA BY INSPIRE, AN ADDUCENT NONFICTION IMPRINT.

ADDUCENT, INC.
JACKSONVILLE, FLORIDA
WWW.ADDUCENTCREATIVE.COM

CONTENTS

DEDICATION & ACKNOWLEDGMENT

This book is dedicated to Sela Gaude. I set out on this journey to write this book while impacting the lives of others. These have been dreams of mine for a long time and would've never been possible without Sela pushing me. Her dedication and daily work got us to the finish line. She helped me stay focused and added comic relief when needed. Without Sela, this manuscript would never have been possible; I am eternally thankful.

I am incredibly grateful to Alex Perry for coming in at the ninth inning and providing invaluable counsel to complete this publication.

Thank you to John C. Maxwell for the inspiration, friendship, and mentorship. You have inspired me to follow my goals, dreams, and aspirations. I am also grateful to you for contributing to the foreword to this book, giving me professional credibility that will impact others. I am blessed to call you my friend.

FOREWORD

Success is an innate desire, yet it eludes many in life. My experience has taught me that life is 10% of what happens to you and 90% how you react to it. Brett K. Oubre has discovered valuable success principles through personal and professional hardships that will inspire everyday people who feel stuck in the middle to attain unimaginable success. *12 Steps to Boundaryless Success* will provide real, relevant, and practical steps to achieving goals and obtaining success.

—John C. Maxwell

Knowing Brett K. Oubre for several decades, I have witnessed his ability to move forward and his desire to lead others with him. Brett passionately believes success is a process, not just an event or a couple of attempts. Success requires a series of deliberate steps leading to goal accomplishments and well-being. *Twelve Steps to Boundaryless Success* is a game changer. It is an exciting, highly engageable read outlining the execution you need to find your way forward! Now that you've taken the first step (by reading the book) make the commitment to follow these life-changing concepts.

—Bryan Flanagan, CEO, Flanagan Training Group
Former Director of Corporate Training, Zig Ziglar

INTRODUCTION

While writing this book has taken me over two years, more than fifty-three years of evaluated experiences have taught me the lessons I will share. My mentor and friend, John Maxwell, refers to the term "evaluated experience" as those life events we learn from by reflecting on what we learned from the experience and applying that knowledge to future decisions. Experience is not the best teacher; *evaluated* experience is the best teacher. Reflective thinking is needed to turn experience into insight.

I think I have a unique and interesting collection of evaluated experiences, and I am very passionate about sharing my success story with others. I grew up with few financial resources (although my parents provided everything my brothers and I needed to survive) and, by implementing the twelve-step process described in this book, worked my way to owning six successful car dealerships and managing over 400 employees—all the while overcoming alcoholism, battling a brain tumor, and surviving a plane crash (among other hardships).

Before finding my calling in the car dealership business, I held countless other jobs, including a line cook at Wendy's and Burger King, a janitor, a door-to-door Christmas card salesman, a yardman, a newspaper deliverer, and a housekeeper—just to name a few. In my twenties, I began my corporate career as a salesperson and eventually transitioned to a business development director. Years later, after experiencing some success, I left my corporate career and bought into a car dealership with seven others. Eventually, I got into commercial real estate development, which was always a dream of mine. My company built over two million square feet of retail across five states. Then in 2013, after experiencing a health crisis, I sold one business I had developed to purchase a car dealership, eventually acquiring five more.

My path to success was not easy. Reflecting on my journey and experiences, I realize there is no roadmap to success. No road signs in life tell you which route to take. Discover your own. The good news is you can learn how to do just that. I hope reading this book will help you find the path leading to your version of success.

—Brett

STEP ONE
REIMAGINE YOURSELF

You are worthy of experiencing Boundaryless Success.

Do you believe that there is always a way forward? There is, but you must be able to trust that before you can find it.

Many books or influencers promise to change, transform, and guarantee success. Like myself, you have probably given in to one or more of their irresistible sales pitches. We sign up, we buy into it, and we subscribe. As a man with decades of sales experience, I should know better than to buy into these quick fixes. Yet, I, too, have invested in programs that did not deliver the expected and "guaranteed" results.

Sometimes, I have listened to a speaker or read a book that offered a fresh perspective and an inspiring new conviction motivated me. I suddenly felt the overwhelming sensation that I CAN DO THIS! But, often, that feeling was short-lived. What usually occurred after the euphoric experience from the inspirational stories and energy was I discovered that I was stuck in the middle of *where I was* and *where I desired to be*. I desperately sought a clear and practical path to personal success but couldn't find the right tools to create one.

Have you ever found yourself in this position? Since you're reading this book, I bet you have shared a similar experience in your pursuit of success.

I get it. Yes, even as the author of this book on success, I understand the yearning for more in life. I have hungered to experience a level of success that seems out of reach. I craved success that would shut down the naysayer in my mind, claiming there was no way forward. I wrote *The 12 Steps to Boundaryless Success* mainly to help you find *your* way by leveraging my mistakes and lessons. I have rebounded from failing, feeling—and being—stuck, and everything in between before reaching success. I hope to help you do the same. I will share the steps taken… and the lessons I learned throughout this book. It is my goal that you take this information and apply it to your daily life.

However, my definition of "success" may look different from yours. In fact, your definition of success *should* be different from mine because we all have different motivations that drive us and differing visions for our futures. Also, it is important to remember that success is not defined by wealth; it is reached by finding your full potential, and only you can determine what you can achieve. One of the biggest hindrances to finding your true potential comes from comparing yourself to others, taking their versions of success, and believing yours should look the same. I am here to help you achieve your version by helping you look within yourself to form a plan and carry it out.

While this book will hopefully motivate you, it is not meant to be a pep talk. This book should eliminate any mystical ideas about reaching goals and give you 12 practical steps to achieve Boundaryless Success. I'll share these proven principles with you, but it requires your action to use them so they take root in your life. No magical experience is promised. However, you can create magic when properly applying my words, thoughts, and ideas. Committing to the process will make you feel motivated, adequately equipped, and ready to find your way forward.

To begin, let's discuss a term that has become vital in my pursuit of reaching my full potential: Boundaryless Success.

WHAT IS BOUNDARYLESS SUCCESS?

Boundaryless Success means there is no limit to where you can go or what you can achieve. It doesn't imply you won't encounter obstacles, just that you can overcome them. Boundaryless Success begins in the imagination and is realized through execution.

When you hear "Boundaryless Success," who do you think of? What names come to your mind? Do you think of celebrities, local heroes, politicians, or other well-known people?

Do you think of yourself?

I bet you might think, *"Not me. What have I done that could fit in that category?"* or, *"I don't have enough money, accomplishments, education, or influence to be considered a person of that caliber."* The list of self-doubting thoughts could continue on and on.

Do you see what just happened there?

These are what I call low self-esteem moments. Why doesn't it feel natural to envision ourselves when we hear the term *Boundaryless Success*? Who told you it is only for a select few? Although we haven't defined the word yet, we assume it doesn't apply to us.

> More often than not, it is easier to see and appreciate others while we continue to devalue ourselves.

Self-doubt and these low self-esteem moments happen when we don't see ourselves as capable. I know all too well about this way of thinking. When I was younger, I delayed success because I believed *people like us don't get to places like that*. I first had to free myself from this negative self-image to achieve my goals and recognize my potential. I want to show you how to do the same.

It is important to note that Boundaryless Success is not a place. Instead, it is an opportunity that we all can experience! It is accessible to you, no matter your background and despite your history, experiences, and challenges.

Everyone is capable of success. But if anyone can succeed, why doesn't everyone just do it? Are there people who would consciously choose to be unsuccessful? The answer is yes because many decide not to try due to the possibility of failure. Here's the thing: the lack of success isn't a direct choice… but it is the result of choices made.

For example, perhaps you dream of earning six figures. Still, you choose not to pursue training, development, or mentorship to increase your strengths and expand your knowledge. In addition, you haven't researched any opportunities for advancement within your current occupation or explored a new one. You never directly said, "I desire to be unsuccessful." However, you decided not to take action to support your dream. Because of those choices, you were unsuccessful in attaining your goal. Our choices and execution are the catalysts in our successes or failures … they directly impact our ability to reach our goals. You can achieve success if you believe you can… and if you act.

The 12 steps outlined in this book will give you proven principles to go from *I can't* to *I can* and *I won't* to *I will*.

Unfortunately, in this world, so much talent and potential are held hostage by how we feel about ourselves. Millions of people across the globe feel unqualified, unequipped, or unworthy of the concept of Boundaryless Success because of how they see themselves.

Please allow me to set the record straight. It does not matter what ethnicity you are, what language you speak, what family you are born into, or your current economic status; YOU ARE WORTHY.

I also recognize that some might have once had a strong sense of purpose and confidence until something caused them to question everything they once believed to be true. This could be divorce, bankruptcy, termination, significant financial loss, criminal convictions, bad credit, or failure, to name a few. The result of this thinking can create a different type of limitation where they feel disqualified from experiencing Boundaryless Success.

> It is important to understand and accept that there is nothing that can disqualify you from getting what you want in life if you are willing to believe in yourself and do the work.

The only person who can prevent you from achieving success is you. You do not have to be a superstar or the founder and CEO to experience incredible success. It will come when you operate at a high level to be the best version of yourself!

> Tap into the unexplored aspects of your potential and give it permission to manifest through self-confidence. Unaddressed issues with comparison will result in mediocrity in your life.

To avoid the trap of comparison, do not allow the success of others to discourage you from believing in your abilities.

Envisioning Boundaryless Success should invoke a mental picture of confidence, hope, endless possibilities, and limitless opportunities. Have you forgotten what hope looks and feels like? There once was a time when you had hope-filled visions. Go back to being a child. Remember how to dream again. Now let's take a moment to close our eyes and remember the last time we had hope. At what age did you stop dreaming or using your imagination? What caused the light to go out? Was it an event, a circumstance, or was it self-inflicted? Regardless of the reason, think about the feelings, events, and actions accompanying your hope-filled imagination as a child. Now let's tap into that hope and start dreaming again, returning to that wonder and optimism. Let's relight that spark!

The originator of the wildly successful *Chicken Soup for the Soul* book series, Jack Canfield, said, "self-esteem is made primarily of two things: feeling lovable and feeling capable." Your self-esteem plays a significant role in your ability to attain new levels of success. But when your self-perception is clouded by the limited view of your present circumstances or negative experiences, taking the first step toward success can be overwhelming or impossible. Do you think your self-esteem is high? Would you believe you can have high self-esteem in one area of your life but low in another? Take this journey with me to reveal those low areas—they will pay high dividends once we address them.

Improving your self-esteem requires you to reframe your mind and believe you can succeed. I know that doing so is easier said than done. It takes faithfulness and consistency to shift your self-perception toward healthy self-esteem. Are you ready to let go of your self-doubts and realize what you are truly capable of?

SECTION A: BREAKING FREE FROM THE PEOPLE LIKE US FALLACY

We're going to begin this process with a visualization exercise. I want you to relax, turn off all distractions, flip your phone over, and be 100 percent present to prepare your mind to get the most out of this exercise.

Are you ready? Let's get started.

Now, envision yourself embracing your first job opportunity and preparing for your first day. You lay out your clothing, ensure all your grooming is done so nothing is out of place, clean your car, and pack everything you need.

What did you imagine yourself doing?

Can you see yourself successfully operating in the role?

When preparing for a new opportunity, are there recurring patterns or thoughts that create anxieties or fears, such as worrying about who your desk will be next to? Maybe you're wondering how long you'll have to wait for a paycheck or how your new coworkers might treat a newbie? Are you anxious about how you will accomplish the task with the shortcomings you didn't disclose or acknowledge, even to yourself?

Why do you think these fears come into your thoughts?

Is this the first time you've had those fears, or is it a recurring pattern or theme?

Does it give you anxiety or an uneasy feeling in your gut?

These are low-esteem events. These are the thoughts that, all things being equal, continue to plague or interfere with moving forward. How would you feel if you could marginalize or eliminate these feelings related to your ability to execute? Write those feelings—the things you fear that inhibit you—down as I take you through the step to repairing this thought process.

This is where the real work begins.

The *people like us* fallacy is derived from a negative self-image and low self-esteem. With this mindset, people focus on failure and categorize themselves into a particular group. Let's explore these groups a little further.

The successful group versus *the failure group*—If you have low self-esteem, you will categorize yourself in the failure group. This depends on what area of their life they lack self-confidence in. Maybe *people like us* don't get good jobs like that. *People like us* don't get an education like that. *People like us* don't get to move to nice neighborhoods. *People like us* don't get opportunities to run companies. Break out of this mindset by intentionally bringing people into your circle of influence in the areas where you have low esteem. Surround yourself with people who do not subscribe to such generalizations and have broken free from this fallacy. You need to see that *people like them* have achieved what wouldn't be possible if they had subscribed to the *people like us* belief.

Honestly, I spent a good portion of my adolescent life filtering my life's possibilities through my current circumstances. I wanted to achieve higher goals but remained stuck by the inner voice that continually doubted my ability to break free. I absolutely knew I was capable of more. Still, I convinced myself that reaching my capability wouldn't be possible because of this gnawing self-doubt. Have you found yourself confident in a situation only to recoil in the face of opposition by allowing self-doubt to sabotage it?

Self-esteem is equated to how you view yourself. You may feel competent, but the voice of self-doubt lowers how you see yourself on that subject and how it will translate to the result.

Now let's take those things you wrote that are stopping you from attempting opportunities. What's the underlying reason they are gnawing at you? Is it fear? Is it relevant now, or is it from a past failure? Was the failure because of a lack of preparation, mindset, or exposure to doubt in other areas? Most gnawing, gut-wrenching things that lower our self-esteem derive from fear, so we must break down why that is.

Lack of preparation. Are you under-prepared or over-prepared? Both can generate a form of fear, leading to lower self-esteem. When we lack preparation, we know it's a laziness issue. We lack the confidence to prepare, so we can generate an excuse when we fall short. Over-preparing has some similarities. Self-doubt can often be so high that the over-preparation results in second-guessing exactly what we know to be true. Do you do any of this? I bet you are imagining a time right now.

Mindset. Do you desire to make life happen or just let it happen to you? Remember, we are still working under the assumption that something is troubling you, although you feel capable of achieving so much more. When I desire to make life happen without clearing my self-doubt, it reverses me back to the moment before I started eradicating the concerns I had. Can you think of a time you took charge, then, as you encountered self-doubt, you were less enthusiastic than before you started? Did you think the idea was wrong? Did you question whether you should have a take-charge attitude? What did this do to your overall self-esteem? What about when you let life happen to you? Have there been times, or are you currently in that cycle, where you don't approach life with intentionality? How does that make you feel? Is there a feeling of anxiety? Does it add to the sense of inadequacy? Go back to the exercise on thinking about your first day. Do you remember the excitement and the fears? These are the self-esteem moments that slowly dim the light of excitement.

Exposure to other areas of your life. Have you evaluated success and failure through a can-do lens? We are who we are because of our experiences, environment, attitude, and evaluation of them, good or bad. Think about the last time excitement faded after starting with endless possibilities. Have there been other times when this has happened to you, or was this a onetime event? If so, what's the recurring theme or thought process? Do you see a pattern developing here? With all three, we continue highlighting the original self-doubt that eats at us. Different things activate it, but what happens if we deal with it? What happens when we do? Could this be the start of Boundaryless Success?

So how is this accomplished? It begins with changing the way we see ourselves. Just humor me for a moment and return to the thoughts about the first day. When the self-doubt started, what could we have done to chase it out? I experienced this as it related to sales. I continued to train myself, get product knowledge, make prospect lists, and get my desk prepared. However, the gnawing self-doubt would creep in when it was time to start. I did as most people would; I froze in fear many times in different opportunities until I reached the point where my back was against the wall. I was struggling just to provide myself with life's necessities.

Are you there in your story yet?

If so, here's how to conquer it:

PREPARE

Proper preparation won't remove self-doubt, but it will get you in a position to start.

Have you ever witnessed a professional at work? They probably asked you questions before presenting you with a cure or plan. What do you think goes into asking those questions? Would you consider this their preparation? How do you think either of you would feel about confidence without preparation? The recipient would discount what was being said, and the professional would come across as shaky and incredibly unsure, which erodes trust in his or her ability. Do you think this would ignite self-doubt in the professional? Do you think that happens to you when you don't prepare? Proper preparation allows for progress when self-doubt attempts to set in. That doesn't mean you will never experience fear, but you'll have the tools to continue.

How do you prepare?

- Read what you need training on until you can repeat the material.
- Write the material over and over until you can do it without notes.
- Speak the materials, recording them until it comes to you without notes.

MAKE YOUR CIRCLE INTENTIONAL

Do you have people in your life who affirm your vision or people who plant seeds of doubt?

Have you ever been telling someone about your plans only to have them bring up every reason they wouldn't work despite your enthusiasm? Did it make you excited, angry, or discouraged? We become an average of the five people we spend the most time with. To conquer self-doubt, we must intentionally place people in our circle who will encourage us rather than tear us down. Having someone encourage you when you haven't prepared is not what I am referring to, but rather people who know your potential and are happy to see you accomplish it. Be intentional with who you share the information. Bringing the wrong people into your circle is like a single cancer cell growing; it will grow out of control before being detected. Will this repair your self-esteem? No, it's primarily an internal job. However, it does limit the discouragement to only what comes from yourself—and we'll tackle that in a moment.

So, how do you surround yourself with a quality circle? First, here are some questions you should ask yourself:

1. Are they growing?

> People that aren't growing will attempt to pull you down as you go up. They get stuck comparing themselves to you, knowing that they are capable of much more as they see you striving to do more.

Can you really encourage someone when you are internally offended by comparison? In contrast, growers are looking to rise as they lift themselves up. You must surround yourself with people who are growing.

2. Are they ahead of you? How will you push yourself through your insecurities if you see people at your level doing the same thing you're doing? You must find people ahead of you who have also traveled the self-doubt path. You think that's rare? It

will surprise you, as more people are stationed in self-doubt than not.

3. Will they encourage you? Can you get motivation from someone who is not encouraging? In your moments of self-doubt, you'll need encouragement from those who have successfully navigated that path.

KEEP GOING

What is going to happen when you get started with your tremendous enthusiasm? Invariably, at some point, self-doubt sets in. I mentioned previously that when it was time for me to make sales calls, I experienced crippling self-doubt. These doubts were the same feelings that had held me back most of my life. I could see the walls closing in as the voice of doom whispered to me, validating the same fears from the beginning. Fortunately, this time was different because my desire to be successful and the basic need to survive made me respond differently by keeping me going when I felt like I couldn't do it. Guess what happened when I kept going? After years of hearing *no*, I got my first *yes*. What did that yes do for me? It started my little wins.

That *yes* quieted the self-doubting voice muttering in my head. As I continued to go, I got more and more yeses. My preparation improved, and the pointers that I got from my inner circle were invaluable. I proved myself and could even offer my circle seeds of wisdom they could grow from. Will this process work for you? I have since successfully mentored many people through self-doubt using this process. You must start by truly believing in yourself. A bonus is that now you have someone else who believes in you, too—me!

As undesirable as some aspects of my life were during that period, I still chose to use those circumstances to create an invisible limitation on my imagination and potential. Although I always felt capable of more, I struggled constantly with feelings of mediocrity.

And being mentally bound to mediocrity results in leading a mediocre life.

> Our life accomplishments will never exceed the boundaries of our imagination.

As a kid who struggled to fit in, I didn't understand this principle. However, as a man who has overcome many failures, I now understand the importance and power of a positive self-image. Truly breaking free from the limits that the *people like us* fallacy puts on your life begins with our imagination.

> Our imagination is a direct product of our self-esteem.

Essentially, this means that we imagine what we believe. If you can't or won't believe something, it will be nearly impossible to imagine beyond that. As a young boy, I struggled to understand that I was capable of Boundaryless Success. I had great parents and came from a good family. I was smart, but I still fought to believe I was worthy. My self-esteem became low; I felt I didn't fit in. I was overweight, wore outdated clothing and shoes, and had a lot of interests typically only attractive to adults—like reading the *Wall Street Journal*. I had no friends and didn't belong to a group like most other kids. I don't mention that for your pity but rather to relate to anyone with a similar experience. I took criticism from people personally because I constantly criticized myself in my head. So, other people's criticism simply reaffirmed the negative voices I already heard in my mind. When I did the work I am describing in this step to free my imagination from the constraints of my fears, I saw clearly the limitless possibilities that my life, talents, and abilities could produce. I confidently empowered my vision and improved my self-esteem with commitment, courage, and consistency. Is any of this resonating with you?

Now that we have discussed Boundaryless Success, I will explain how I freed my imagination by repairing my self-esteem.

SELF-ESTEEM'S ROLE IN SUCCESS

The American Psychology Association (APA) defines self-esteem as "the degree to which the qualities and characteristics in one's self-concept are perceived to be positive. It reflects a person's physical self-image, view of accomplishments, capabilities, values, and perceived success in living up to them, as well as how others view and respond to that person."

Beloved author Mark Twain described the importance of self-esteem by stating, "A man cannot be comfortable without his own approval." I like the depth and detail of the APA's definition, but I also appreciate the simplicity Mark Twain's statement offers. The point of both is to ensure that you and I are on the same page regarding the meaning of self-esteem and how it relates to achieving Boundaryless Success.

My version of self-esteem is simple: it's how people think about themselves, their talents, skills, and abilities. Self-esteem comes from within—from the heart and the mind. Most people with broken self-esteem are fearful, reluctant, or unable to follow through on their wants. They stay in their comfort zones and never stretch out of them. How do I know? Because I once was one of those people.

- I lived in a lower-income neighborhood.
- I didn't wear the best clothes.
- I struggled with my weight as an adolescent.
- I had different hobbies than other children my age.
- I struggled with how people perceived me.

What I just shared is not at all an exhaustive list. I share these parts of my life to let you know I am not this wealthy old guy who's out of touch with the struggle. I get it. Evidently, I had to endure these experiences to reach success in my life. I started from humble beginnings as a child to working ten years as a young man, to owning several successful businesses and employing hundreds of people as an adult.

Before I could enjoy any type of success, I had to repair how I thought about who I was and what I could do.

It is my belief that self-esteem's role in success is imperative. Why? Because in my opinion, self-esteem is the bedrock of our motivation, discipline, and actions in life. It is the internal permission granter when it comes time to execute and persevere during difficult times. Self-esteem is our compass when we feel lost. It gives us encouragement when we face challenges. I view it as an invisible leader that our actions follow.

Former first lady, Michelle Obama, has a profound thought on self-esteem: "Your success will be determined by your own confidence and fortitude."

How do you view self-esteem's role in success?

Is self-esteem a leader or a follower?

I encourage you to consider and write your answers as we explore these ideas.

WHERE DOES SELF-ESTEEM DERIVE FROM?

Many believe that resources, perfect families, or good luck determine who will succeed. My life experiences have shown me that self-esteem is the first foundational step in Boundaryless Success.

In my research, I located this description on the Abalance Client-Centered Counseling blog of where self-esteem derives from: "Self-esteem is based on who you are and the relationships and experiences you have had at home, in school, with friends, and in the community. You form an image of yourself based on these experiences and relationships. Positive experiences and relationships contribute to healthy self-esteem, and negative experiences and relationships contribute to poor self-esteem."

High self-esteem is an intangible and invaluable quality inside a person's mind and heart. It is a quality that we are all born with. When cultivated healthily, it can contribute to a life filled with personal and professional success. In a perfect world, we would all grow from infants to adults with iron-clad confidence in our worth, talents, purpose, and strengths. But that is not the case for most. Many experience life in a way that does not build self-esteem but challenges it.

Low self-esteem: fear, doubt, anxiety, overthinking, or lack of action.

High self-esteem: confidence, risk-taking, determination, and resourcefulness.

It is important to take note a person can have areas where they have higher self-esteem than others. There are also times when we experience low-esteem moments but can quickly bounce back in confidence.

Example: I have high self-esteem in managing employees, financial management, social interaction, etc. However, I deal with low self-esteem daily concerning weight management and the mental and physical aspects of controlling my weight. I could say, "screw it," and eat whatever I want whenever I want, but my high self-esteem in other aspects drives me to control those low self-esteem moments. Learning and applying the concepts in this book taught me that my low self-esteem moments do not have to rule my inner thoughts or actions.

Based on my life experiences and research, I believe three key things cultivate self-esteem: relationships, failure, and success. I will break this all down in the following sections of the book. As I share the content, I want you to imagine the two of us—me and you—conversing face-to-face. I'll share personal stories, life lessons, research, and examples to help you gain valuable insights to find your way forward and repair your self-esteem.

THE ROLE OF RELATIONSHIPS IN BUILDING SELF-ESTEEM

Many different relationships work together to build our self-esteem. This section will focus primarily on the parent-child relationship and how a parent's words impact a child's self-esteem. I firmly believe that the origin of self-esteem is cultivated in our upbringing. Imagine a seed in the soil. The tiny seed has so much potential hidden inside. Over time, and with proper cultivation, it will become exactly what it was planted to be. This analogy perfectly depicts what I mean when I say that upbringing is the origin of our self-esteem. And just like seeds, soil types, and plants, growth journeys will differ. The same can be said for self-esteem and how upbringing can lead to future success.

Some people are born into situations they did not choose, such as poverty, violence, abuse, absent parents, traumatic experiences, foster systems, etc. Nothing in this book is intended to be written insensitively or to put each individual person into one bucket. However, embracing what I am saying to you with an open mind as you continue reading this section is important. Some of my information may be challenging or hard to process because of your life experiences. This is my encouragement for you in these cases: do not quit or give up.

Discomfort is proof that you are growing!

I assure you that if you keep pushing forward, you'll experience new levels of success.

Now that we have addressed this critical point, let's dig deeper into how our upbringing affects our self-esteem.

As a father, I now understand parenting isn't the easiest job. So, by no means is this book meant to bash parents. I had great parents. I am sure many of you had great parents too, or you had parents who did their best considering the circumstances. Reexamining your childhood aims to help you move forward in your adult life.

As we explore this thought further, note that when I say *upbringing*, I refer to parental, relational, environmental, societal, educational, and religious interactions that shape our view of ourselves. Whether you had strict or nurturing parents or they were somewhere in between, I know you've been told "no" before.

Even if you came from the wealthiest families and were given all the love in this world, I am confident you've been told "no" before.

THE COMPOUNDING EFFECT OF *NO*

Other than "dada" or "mama," what is one of the first words a baby says? "No!" In defense of the kid, it is a simple, one-syllable word to pronounce. But is that the real reason they say it? Babies say "no" so quickly because they are told it so often. While there is wisdom in saying "no," especially for a baby, it is also a constant subliminal message. The message essentially is *you can't*. Think about it—if your whole first couple years of life are shaped by being told *you can't*, what effect does that have on your budding self-esteem? Hold on to that thought while we dig a little deeper.

The next question I have for you is why there is such a parental focus on *no* rather than focusing on *yes*? Or on "don't do that, don't touch this, and leave that alone" instead of offering positive alternatives like "you can do this, you can touch that, and you can play with that." Again, as a father, I can vouch for the word *no*. In most cases, I use it to protect, prevent, or deter something bad from happening. That's the upside benefit of using no. The downside is that without an equal or greater investment in highlighting what you *can* do, you may subliminally accept *I can't* as a mindset.

Research proves that constant negative feedback can harm a child's healthy development. *Psychology Today* author David Schwartz, LMFT, said, "When [children] are constantly being told they are wrong and aren't living up to your expectations, they don't always understand your intention is to help them do better. Instead, it's easy for them to internalize that you disapprove of them. This may lead them to believe something is fundamentally wrong with them, which can affect their self-image. As a result, how a child is redirected or disciplined can make a big difference in his or her self-esteem." This is why redirecting leads to better long-term results as opposed to reprimanding.

Parental Example: A pastor and a major league baseball player went to a prison to visit the inmates. Everybody was enamored with this baseball player because he was famous. The warden asked him, "how did you know you would be a professional baseball player?" He said, "my dad said to me, 'if you keep that up, you're going to be a major leaguer one day.'" A trustee was standing next to them, cleaning and mopping the floors. Eavesdropping, the trustee leaned in and said, "You know, you're right. My dad told me, 'If you keep doing what you're doing, you're going to wind up in jail one day.'"

I can sense that some of you might think, "that's great, Brett, but what am I supposed to do now? I am xx years old." This moment of awareness is not to sentence you to a lifetime of limited thinking. We got to this point to reveal your way forward. You move forward by mastering the redirection of your thoughts from *I can't* to *I can*. I trust this is not the first time you've heard this encouragement. The difference is that it will make hearing "I can't" and "I can" entirely up to you. Will you decide to get different results, or are you satisfied with your results based on your understanding?

While you think about that, let's continue exploring this train of thought.

SECTION B: DISCONNECTING FROM LIMITATIONS AND RECONNECTING WITH YOUR POTENTIAL

This portion of Step One is when you are empowered to take specific action to repair your self-esteem. If you aren't ready to rebuild your self-esteem, put the book down and continue no further. If you're still following me, it's time to disconnect from your self-doubt and negative self-image.

As we begin, note that I purposely intended for these bullet points to be general to allow you to personalize them. Only you know what you need to let go of in these areas.

What to disconnect from:

- Bad experiences
- Opinions
- Regret
- Guilt
- Shame
- Lies
- Comparison
- Negative self-talk
- Limited beliefs

By disconnecting from this, I mean you must stop doing it. Plain and simple. When limiting thoughts arise, overcoming them requires intentional and consistent action. Instead of succumbing to the negative emotion of the moment, choose to believe in what is possible and act in that area.

What to reconnect to:

- Trusting yourself.
- Believing in yourself.
- Having confidence in yourself.
- Being willing to take risks.
- Acting in accordance with your desires.

We reconnect through trust and belief in our potential by re-engaging positive perceptions of our self-image. Through this reconnection process, you will begin the powerful process of repairing your self-esteem. Doesn't that make much of what we've been going over clearer? I would go even further to say that *we replay what we believe.* So shifting from *I can't* to *I can* requires a disconnect and reconnect.

Disconnect from thinking that you are limited so that you can reconnect to your newfound belief of being capable and worthy.

I get it; life happens. That pure form of confidence has been diluted with things that cause you to question your abilities. Do you realize we have been wired to believe in our potential this way?

Observe a baby maturing into the toddler stage. Everything that they explore is done with so much inner confidence. The risk of failure doesn't appear to be a concern.

Babies crawl.

They climb.

Toddlers say what comes to mind.

They take steps.

They walk.

Do you see the progression of organic self-esteem and confidence? Can you see how you were born to believe in yourself? Believe it or not, we can reconnect to this natural place of trust and healthy self-image. And we will continue this process together.

Here is an important principle I want you to understand: *your upbringing doesn't determine your life's potential—your decisions do.* As we work toward repairing your self-esteem, owning this responsibility is vital.

FAILURE'S ROLE IN SELF-ESTEEM

Most people's self-esteem will take a hit from the F-Word: failure. Failure can feel fatal, but only if you let it. I will help you reframe your thinking to see failure as an ally in building healthy self-esteem. Let's make failure our friend.

In my experience, failure specifically impacts self-esteem based on your mindset.

Example: Low self-esteem provokes thoughts like *I cannot believe I did that. I told you it would not work. I knew this would happen,* or *I knew people like us don't do stuff like this.* Failure can discourage, delay, or destroy someone with low self-esteem. When you have healthy self-esteem, failure has an entirely different effect.

The way the mind works is that it subconsciously goes to work to place items around it to actuate the decision it has already made. If you say, "I am going to be a failure," you will look for situations that agree with that fact. Failure will not negatively affect you if you have positive, healthy self-esteem. Having a positive self-image and a positive outlook on our skill sets, talents, and abilities as they relate to who we are as a person prepares us for weathering the unexpected without losing our identity.

With that being said, failure is bound to happen. I have failed many times. For instance, when I began developing my first shopping center, I put a contract on the land without researching what a shopping center would require regarding water, sewer, and regulatory and construction costs. Long story short, I lost a large amount of money, delaying some of my long-term goals because I failed to fully prepare. This mistake taught me that while an opportunity could be viable… if you don't look into all avenues for identifying the risks to make an informed—calculated—decision, you can deem it a failure when it wasn't. The failure was yours when you didn't prepare.

When I experience failures, I choose first to recognize that I am a good person. I have talents and abilities, but somewhere I made a mistake. What is the lesson here? What can I learn, and what can I apply? Mistakes and failures are a part of my growth and journey rather than a hindrance.

Did you see I didn't lead with the negative even in a moment of failure? Instead, I affirmed my good qualities, which opened the door for me to see failure as an opportunity, not an obstacle. This intentional way of thinking took me time to master, and now that I have, I don't get downtrodden or discouraged by failure. I can seize the opportunity that it creates and find my way forward.

You must get into your conscious mind and out of your subconscious mind (which we will unpack in more depth in Step Two). Say to yourself, "I know my circumstances now, but I will actuate what I want around me. I will not treat this temporary setback as a permanent obstacle. I am going to use it to learn and grow."

I encourage you to choose to have the self-esteem to know that failure doesn't define you while acknowledging that you need self-compassion to let go of unfair expectations. Let go of experiences and trust in your future and your ability to succeed. This decision is within your grasp, irrespective of your previous experiences in life.

What will you decide?

SUCCESS'S ROLE IN SELF-ESTEEM

Hopefully, it is very easy to understand the correlation between success and self-esteem. Without a doubt, success can fuel healthy self-esteem when working within our purpose and talent zone (as we go further, I refer to this area as your *strength zone*). Despite what many may feel, success does not create self-esteem. However, it can vastly increase it.

> Self-esteem is a complete inside job and it can benefit from affirmation and validation after a success, but it is not codependent upon achievements.

Author and behavioral investigator Vanessa Van Edwards said, "True self-worth is more than that. It's the permanent, grounded *knowing* that you have worth. And unlike a cloud, self-worth is more like the earth. It's an unmovable, grounded belief rooted in confidence—and a snide remark or unfortunate circumstance won't destroy your self-worth."

I work with people daily, and I am known for sharing this mantra: Don't chase success; success comes to those *ready for it.* We prepare for success by doing the hard internal work we discuss throughout this book. This work includes developing successful disciplines behind the scenes and remaining focused and persistent in our daily lives without needing immediate gratification. Success directly results from believing in ourselves and being willing to work in concert with that belief.

I want you to realize you can repair your damaged self-esteem through this step. You can fix negative self-talk. If I did it, then you can too. You have something bigger in you. Something greater is out there for you. You can make a positive out of a negative situation and tap into opportunities. You can make failure your friend instead of your enemy. Regardless of what has happened, you have a purpose and can control your thoughts. You can have a pity party and think, "Poor little pitiful me," or you can decide, "I'm going to do more with what I've been given, even though it's been less."

Remember, everyone has two voices in their head: *I can*, and *I can't*. As your self-esteem repairs, you will hear more of the *I can*. Self-esteem is the foundation of positive thinking. It's hard to have clear thinking with broken self-esteem. Repairing your self-esteem begins with the awareness that you don't have to listen to those demons in your head. It is knowing that you are more and can do more despite what you've been told by someone else, despite your upbringing, and regardless of your present circumstances. When you realize this, you can begin your journey toward Boundaryless Success.

Each step to repair your self-esteem requires work; this step starts the process. There are segments and levels to the process; it's not finite. By continuing to read this book, you are planting a seed. I can't give a timeframe for how long the work to repair your self-esteem will take because that depends on what you grasp and will do. This work requires revealing yourself to yourself. You must examine what has gone into your mind until this point to get you to where you want to be.

Though the work is laborious, it's very easy to understand. Still, you must dig into it. You may already know the greatness inside of you but need help to pull it out so you can succeed. You may need a professional counselor to help you with some things. You probably will need to go beyond what you expected. Some days, the work will be great. On other days, it won't. There will be failures along the way. But, if you draw a line… over a year, you'll move forward. At some point, the low self-esteem will be gone, and the work will be worth it, but you must be prepared. The principles in this book will not work for you if you're not prepared to work consistently.

Work starts for you tomorrow. When you wake up in the morning, know what you can do. Wake up knowing that you have great greatness inside of you. Tap into that thing in your heart with a higher purpose and think *I can do this, and I will.*

PRACTICAL STEPS FORWARD

I aim to help you improve your self-esteem to succeed and find your way forward.

We covered a lot in this step, but it all boils down to these four words, *repair your self-esteem* and these five points below.

1. Break free from the *people like us* fallacy.
2. Disconnect from limitations and reconnect to your potential.
3. Envision your future without the limitations of low self-esteem.
4. Plan for the future you imagine and write it down.
5. Take action and don't accept excuses.

STEP TWO
Retrain Your Brain

Everything you think is a reality; it's always the opposite.

How do you train your brain to think differently?

Thinking positively is one of the top drivers of success because your mind decides and executes your decisions. This step is about training your brain to create a new level of thinking.

There are two ways to use your brain to decide: subconsciously or consciously. Most people make subconscious decisions that are not intentional. The non-intentional decision has no action plan behind it and absorbs the world as it comes. However, these decisions are deliberate in that we decide not to choose the direction. Have you ever thought *I just can't seem to achieve,* or *I never get those opportunities?* Have you considered that the reason for this is that there is no conscious intentionality to the direction in which you were headed? Generally, things turn out the way they do because of the plan of execution or the lack thereof. The decision is placed in your control. Conscious decisions require putting a thought process into the desired result, then setting things, people, and resources around you to achieve it. Will you achieve precisely what you want 100 percent of the time? No. However, you will hit the target or get closer to it than with subconscious decision-making.

Let me ask you a few questions: When do you think your thinking turned more subconscious than conscious? What external and internal factors contributed to this switch? Do you remember the last time you had hope?

When we are children, most of us think anything is possible—especially when we have a conscious plan to carry out our decisions and understand what's required to make them happen. Think back to when you were a kid or when your child decided they wanted something and asked, "Can I have XYZ?" often, the response is "Not right now," "Maybe later," or "You don't need that." How do children typically respond to those answers? By telling you why they need it, how it would benefit them or you, or why it is required to improve their life or yours. Do you think they were using their conscious or subconscious? I think we would all agree that although they may not be aware of the concept, they have consciously decided how to manifest what they want to happen. They thought through what obstacles they may face, how to overcome them, and who to enlist to make their desire come true. Now that we have laid that out, you'll have a greater appreciation next time that happens to you. Why do you think most people quit processing conscious decisions and thus let the majority of their lives be led by the subconscious? I believe that while there are many factors, here are some of the most common:

- **Failure.** Our general response is to quit when the result isn't exactly as we imagined.
- **Fear.** When we start a task, we know minimal worry, but when the outcome doesn't match our exact vision, a heavy amount of fear stops us from thinking consciously because we have to hold ourselves accountable and evaluate each assumption that leads to a decision. Still having trouble? Go back and study Step One.

- **Environmental Factors.** Why are people destined to repeat similar lifestyles from where they came from? They have never intimately seen modeling from a trusted person regarding their hopes, dreams, and aspirations. Or they have allowed their environmental situation to shape their thoughts (we will deal with this later.).

When you lack intentionality in decision-making, you will eventually find yourself never actually accomplishing anything you set out to achieve in your career and personal life. The intentional decision-making process will help you set goals and accomplish them.

The difference between being born to think and thinking intentionally is going from subconscious thinking to intentional thinking. Subconscious thinking is your everyday thinking, which involves things you need and want to do. This thinking is based on the here and now; it does not require a thought process but acts as a reflex to satisfy whatever you want or need. Intentional thinking is having a plan of attack on what information you decide to put in your mind and how you will use the information to achieve your goals.

Examples: I want to go get something to eat. I want to go to my friend's house. I need to go to work today. I need to go do this. I need to go do that. Intentional thinking transforms *I want* to *I will* and brings definition to completed tasks. Tell yourself, "I *will* send three emails by 9:00 a.m. today," or "I *will* submit the employment application today by 4:00 p.m." What we think is based mainly on how we view ourselves. Self-esteem is a building block of thinking.

Conscious thinking requires training your brain to create a level of understanding that allows you to reach your goals, dreams, aspirations, and visions for your life. This type of thinking must be intentional, thought-out, and well-planned. To retrain your thinking, you need to create and execute a plan. If you have goals for your life, you need a plan of attack that uses intentional thinking to achieve these goals.

Unfortunately, our thoughts are also shaped by environmental factors, such as the people around us daily. Most people don't realize that they place their circle of influences around them based on their subconscious. If I decide that I'm going to be an overeater, I'm going to put overeaters around me who will not challenge me. They're going to be the ones who say, "It's okay; we can go eat more. You only live once." But, if I consciously decide to focus on my personal fitness, I will bring people around me who are fitness-oriented. If I overeat, they're going to antagonize that behavior. I'm conscious and mentally mature enough to know that fitness is a goal, dream, aspiration, and vision for my life, so I will put people who will challenge me in those areas.

FEED YOUR BRAIN FOR SUCCESS

Everyone knows that if you feed your body with healthy food, it will function better. The same applies to your brain. Your brain is not just a twenty-four-hour-a-day working robot that you have no influence or control over. What you allow into your mind, intentionally or unintentionally, determines your thoughts. Consider dreams. Have you ever watched something scary or received terrible news late at night? How easy is it to find rest? How does this affect your dreams? Most people struggle with sleeping well after receiving this information or entertainment late at night. Why? Because their brain has been fed information that is now affecting their thoughts. This does not just happen at night; this happens early morning, midday, and late afternoon. While you cannot control unexpected events, you can control what you invest your time, energy, and focus on. Feeding your brain success is something that I have focused on for decades. It is a habit that I remain disciplined in, no matter how successful I've become. I purposely and consistently feed my brain positive thoughts, new words, leadership principles, and other positive tools to maintain a strong mindset. A person who lacks a healthy perspective is unable to grow.

I discovered I needed to change what I was putting into my brain when I understood the correlation between self-esteem and thinking. As I state many times throughout this book, most of my life, I thought I was capable of achieving Boundaryless Success, but I struggled to attain it for years. The struggle directly resulted from what I was feeding my brain then. Subconsciously, I fed my brain thoughts like, *You don't fit in, you're just a poor, overweight kid, you can't do things like that,* and *how could someone with your background achieve success on that level?*. My negative subconscious reality was revealed in my daily decisions and actions. This way of thinking kept me stuck wanting things in life without the confidence to take steps to pursue those wants. Failure after failure produced a pain that screamed for change. I knew if I truly believed I was capable of more, then something must change. That change began with working on my thinking. While I had a lot of negative thoughts swirling in my subconscious, it was not my goal to get rid of them. My goal was to chase out negative thoughts the moment they started. I began by identifying them and focusing on the solutions rather than the problem that created the negative thinking. By focusing on the positive, you'll organically eliminate the negative.

My journey started by developing a plan of action for my life because anything with a target has a better opportunity to succeed. Then, I began identifying people I admired and could learn from through books and other platforms. Next, I took control of my day by developing a healthy morning routine. Afterward, I created a system for success by executing my daily task toward my goals, including accountability and personal evaluation. Finally, I executed with no excuses. Even though I didn't start confident, I did not allow myself to use that as an excuse. I began my action plan, which took months to become a solid, consistent part of my life. Meaningful change takes time and cannot happen overnight.

You can relate to my story if you're reading this book. Many of us have felt disgusted, embarrassed, or even ashamed of our lack of progress in life. Or you may feel you're living in shackles and chains. Perhaps you constantly tell yourself, "I can't wait until retirement," "I can't wait until Friday," or "I can't wait until vacation." These types of thoughts are toxic. You're not promised tomorrow or next week. You need to change your thinking because the time is now!

The thinking that you have today has gotten you to where you are. To go somewhere tomorrow, your thinking must evolve. This will require your intentional effort to feed your brain the information it needs to grow and thrive.

RETRAINING YOUR BRAIN TO BECOME AN INTENTIONAL THINKER

Intentional thinking requires understanding what materials you will put in your mind. One way to accomplish this is by listening to motivational podcasts or talks about your goals. Fill your mind with research and resources related to your plan.

As an intentional thinker, I list what I want to achieve. Then I put materials into my head that reinforce that thinking rather than concentrating on thoughts that just pop into my head and deter my focus. The same approach goes for reading materials. I'm intentional in what I read. Whether it's articles, publications, or programs I'm watching on a computer or television, they are intentionally centered on what will pour information into my mind that facilitates a plan I've already decided to execute.

Many people don't realize that the mind is a muscle. It must be exercised, or it stops growing. The mind decides if you're going to move your leg. The mind decides if you're going to move your arm. The mind decides how you're going to react when you're driving. The mind decides if you will be anxious and sad or happy, in a good mood, and ready to give it your all. All those actions and emotions come from the mind, yet most people let the subconscious decide, so you have to switch from the subconscious to the conscious.

> Growing in your desired direction requires your mind to grow as well.

Becoming an intentional thinker requires a few steps. Depending on where you are now will determine where you start. The first step is understanding what is driving your current thought process. You must evaluate your thinking in the following areas: health, finances, relationships, professional goals, and personal situation. You should ask yourself, "What is my thinking today based on?" and "What do I want to accomplish in each area in life?" Imagine, "What does success in these areas look like?"

Secondly, you want to create a vision for improving in those areas. Envision just how you will improve. Answer the questions, "What do I want to improve?" and "Where am I trying to go in each area?" Obviously, if you're reading this book, you want improvement.

The third step is putting a plan together that includes goals of intentionally feeding your brain with the materials that will rewire your thinking. Once you have a plan, review it often to make necessary changes and increase your chances of success.

Intentional thinking is a trial-and-error process, and not everything will come to fruition (which is okay and simply a part of the process). As you go down that road to rewiring your thinking, some things won't work out how you thought they would. Mentally, break things apart and analyze what happened:

- What did you learn?
- What can you grow from?
- What lessons can you apply moving forward?
- Who can you contact with a different perspective to help develop your thinking?
- What materials can you listen to that will help you apply these thoughts?

The fourth and final step is executing that plan. The most important step is starting! When you start growing your mind, you don't know what you don't know, but by Step Four, you know what you didn't know. Getting new ideas without ever starting only increases your frustration level. At some point, you must take action while evaluating what can be learned and applied, then continue moving forward. If you grow your mind but never begin, you're worse off than the person who did nothing because now you know what you don't know, but you frustratingly won't take action.

MAKE THE SWITCH

You need to consume and understand the information before you start, but you must move forward from subconscious living to intentional living. A friend helped me to understand the need to act. A dream of mine was to work in commercial real estate development. I got the idea in high school when I had a job filing paperwork at an insurance company; the owner's son was a commercial real estate developer. I used to go to his office to empty the trash cans in the evening. I noticed his plans and drawings of things he was building in our local area in the trash can. Looking at those made me think I wanted to do some form of development as a secondary career.

Years later, I had a business next door to six acres of vacant land. I thought building a shopping center on the vacant property would be great, so I called my friend in Los Angeles two or three times a week to tell him all my great ideas about the shopping center. He had done some development work, and, in my mind, I was trying to get him to tell me the step-by-step process of success to remove the uncertainty, fear, and anguish I felt. I was trying to get him to make me feel like I had no risk moving forward—after all, he was the expert. I was trading my mind activity for productivity because I thought I was moving the idea forward by calling him, but I wasn't. I was gathering all the information but wasn't doing anything with it. I'll never forget one day when I called him, and he said, "You've called five or six times on the same topic. Don't call me back until you've taken action." Then he hung up on me. The next day, I put a purchase agreement on the land. Today, a shopping center sits there. Though the project took much longer than expected, I got it done and learned many lessons.

From when I had the idea to buy the vacant land until the closing of the purchase, I was putting all kinds of information in my head. Like me, people often have something specific they want to do and have been thinking about for a while. Maybe they want to lose weight, so they read weight-loss articles. Maybe they want to eat healthily, but they keep putting it on the back burner because they know there will be pain associated and sacrifices required. They find every reason to put off the risk of attempting to accomplish a goal. Unfortunately, I've often seen it with health. Some people have a health scare, inspiring them to research all the information to change their health path. Yet, their health continues to decline because no action is ever taken. At some point, you must act.

I started growing my mind over twenty years ago when I started a new sales job. I realized I needed to professionally retrain my brain at a corporate meeting. I was listening to a gentleman speak about various categories: finances, personal relationships, and health—physical, mental, and spiritual. He said, "You should have a plan in each one of those areas in your life." I'd never heard that before. At that time, I had no plan for my life.

Until then, I took life as it was coming and didn't have any action plan. I knew I *needed* a job. I knew I *needed* a car. I knew I *needed* a place to live, but I had no action plan. I had no idea what my future looked like three to seven years later. If I had stayed on that path, which is where many people are, I would have woken up at fifty years old in that same position. If I could rewind and talk to the person from before, I would have made that decision earlier.

At that time, I just went through life with thoughts such as, *That would be a good thing to do,* or *This would be a good thing to do.* My experiences were the sum of my thinking at that time. My life situations were based on my subconscious thought. My approach was, *You want to go get a job? That'd be great! Let me go get this job.* But nothing was planned to get that job, and nothing was designed to reach the goals of that job. Instead, I thought, *I will go to work every day and hope everything works out.*

When I returned to my hotel room that night after hearing the gentleman speak at the meeting, I realized I needed a plan. Then, I had to execute it on a daily, weekly, and monthly basis if I was going to see any improvement in my life. I had to be intentional about what I was doing. So, that night, I wrote my plan out for each one of those areas and went to work every day doing those things. If you think back to any time you decided to work toward a goal, whether it was taking a school course, changing some situation, losing weight, exercising daily, or having a better relationship, the day you really made the change was different from every other. You felt different because you mentally convinced yourself, *Today's the day. Today is going to be different.* You knew it was going to be different from before.

For me, that night in the hotel room, I knew my life would be different because I was committed to making a change. I'd had enough pain at that point because my subconscious thinking had failed me. Had it failed me as a person? No, but I was stuck in mediocrity. I went to work. I had achieved some things. I had gathered some things materially, but it failed me because I knew I could do much more than what I was doing. Still, I didn't know how to connect the dots to reach the next level. I was frustrated daily because I felt stuck. I often thought *this is an okay opportunity, but it's not great. It's not what I'm capable of.* But I knew that night that hearing about setting goals in areas of my life and then deciding to do something would change me forever. I was right! Though I had just taken on this sales job, I told myself, "I'm going to become the best salesperson I can be."

I realized that to make that happen, my thinking must transform. I found relatable and applicable reading materials and committed to reading an hour daily in my first two targeted growth areas—sales and motivation. I told myself that I would not listen to music anymore. Podcasts didn't exist back then, so I bought CDs and tapes to listen to in the car. At the time, I traveled a long distance to get to work. So, when I got into my vehicle, instead of an empty time feeding my brain music and subliminal messages, I intentionally put what I was trying to accomplish in my mind. A segment of my driving time was devoted to each area I wanted to improve. I had heard that if you're going to become an expert on anything, you must read an average of one hour a day on the subjects for five years, so I took advantage of my long commute to hear information on topics I wanted to become an expert in.

I had information to make me a better person, employee, and salesperson. I bought a CD from a motivational speaker who valued being the right kind of person, going to work on a regular schedule, getting up every morning, and being polished and ready to go. I took a notebook to work and wrote down the sales lessons as I was learning them. As I made my sales calls daily, I practiced what I read in front of people. As I practiced what was in the sales book, I followed a tried-and-true field person who had already done it. I started seeing results from my actions, which gave me the confidence to say, "I'm really doing this. This is working."

I also realized that I needed to read, write, and speak about the new things I was putting into my mind. I knew my mind was growing, and by doing these things regularly, I retrained my subconscious mind based on what I consciously put in it. From that point forward, everything seemed different—and I suspect that will happen to you too.

Before I started these new plans and practices, my sales were sporadic. While I had overcome the fear of making the call, I didn't have a plan. I simply got in the car and made calls to see what would happen. Once I started growing my skill set, I started understanding how to set up a sales call, do a needs analysis, prospect someone properly, figure out their desires, needs, and expectations to see if our program was a good fit for them, and finally, to help them visualize it. Despite all that new information, I often still got to a point where I felt I wasn't succeeding. However, I could analyze my process because I had grown my thinking: Am I doing the basics? Am I visualizing the decision maker (the person deciding whether to purchase my product)? Is my presentation perfect? Am I asking the right questions when I talk to the decision maker? Am I going down the road to the sale? Am I making it about the customer? Am I being persistent and painting the visual picture? I had information to process and evaluate the situation. I switched from external evaluation to internal.

When I experienced failure before that point, I always blamed external factors. The old me would say, "It must be the market. It must be the time of year. It must be them because I'm so well-equipped that there's no way that it's me." Subconscious thinking will fail you because the subconscious will look for external factors to blame for the lack of execution. People who do not achieve desired success view the world this way and develop an *It Can't Be Me* response. The reason they don't reach their goals becomes an external reason: "I didn't become the teacher I wanted to become because I didn't have the opportunity to go to school. My parents didn't have that kind of money." Yet, we could find somebody with a similar or worse situation who was accomplishing those things. The irony of life is that for every person who says they can't and won't, you can find an example of somebody who did and then did more. When my thinking is not growing, the subconscious always looks for an external factor to blame... anybody but myself.

If you stay in the subconscious, it's going to create pain and disappointment.

Typically, people who think subconsciously have no plan for their life and are simply taking the world as it comes, which is how I lived for a long time. More often than not, people unknowingly live in the subconscious because, at some point, in a conscious moment, they had a list of things they wanted to do. Still, fear, uncertainty, and lack of commitment caused them to suppress their goals because they didn't want to put the work in. Everyone has fears, but people paralyzed by fears feel they're the only ones with them. They see people accomplish things and think they aren't scared of anything. People who stay in the subconscious just show up. While their intentions may be good and pure, showing up unprepared produces no results.

Before switching from the subconscious to intentional thinking, I would never ask, "How can I apply the information I am learning to improve?" when I face failure. When I added it up and put practices into play, I began to see a new me. I realized I didn't have to have low self-esteem events because I had a new way of thinking. I recognized what I did and why I did it. My goals are still not impossible. I can go back to the visualization and make new plans. With intentional thinking, I have a list of things I will do and hold myself accountable for hitting the mark.

Not only did I see the positive results daily at work with my new way of thinking and daily actions, but I also started seeing the results in my paycheck. I started seeing the results in my home life because as I became more successful and grew my mind, I became happier. My professional and personal relationships suddenly improved, even though I did nothing different in those relationships. But my thinking was different, and I was different. I began to like who I was.

Next, I began focusing on my health and started losing weight. I started feeling better and having more energy. All these positive changes were based on what I fed my mind intentionally daily. I became more interested in the books, CDs, and growth materials that fed my mind. When some of the changes I made did not produce the desired result, I reevaluated and continued focusing on the lessons I was learning during the process.

During this time, I learned a key principle: when you're growing your mind and growing as a person, you're much happier than when you're contracting. In life, you're either expanding or contracting; there's no treading water. People who claim, "I'm not a person of growth," are going backward because if you're not improving, you're going backward. When somebody says, "I'm not a person of change," that person doesn't recognize that the world changes whether you evolve with it or get left behind.

Everything changes daily. If you don't believe me, return to the neighborhood you lived in ten years ago; it's different now. Interview the people you were around as a child and see if they've stayed the same or gotten better or worse. Everybody either goes forward or backward.

I reached my career goal within one year of growing into this new version of myself. I became the number one salesperson in that company. Though I had experienced some success in sales, I had never experienced any success at that high level. The accomplishment was even more significant because the company had debated putting a salesperson in that market area (we worked for a technology firm, and they didn't think rural Louisiana was where they should place someone).

In this process of intentional thinking, visualization is critical for successfully engaging your mind to move toward your goals. Once you set specific goals, you have to literally see yourself accomplishing them by visualizing what success looks like in your mind. Most people say, "I want to lose weight," but never imagine their life once the weight is gone. They can't imagine the confidence and energy that accompanies not being overweight.

When I have a health goal, I visualize what the success of that goal looks like. It might be, "I want to be at 175 pounds; I want to have three percent body fat." Beyond the goal, I need to envision what I look like in that perfect outfit. I need to have a vision of myself going on that perfect date or going with my children and having an ideal visualization of where we're going and what I look like and feel. I visualize how I'm going to feel in my mind when I achieve that goal. I imagine how compliments are going to come and how confident I'm going to be.

To use a professional example, let's say your dream occupation is to be a doctor. First, see yourself in the role of a doctor. You do that by considering having a business card with *MD* on it. You see yourself in a room full of colleagues having medical discussions. You also answer specific questions, like, how do you feel when you're a doctor? What does it look like when you have that professional credibility? How does it feel to see a patient? How does it feel doing surgery? How do you feel when you're around your neighbors, family, or friends, and they ask what you do, and you can say, "I'm a doctor?" How accomplished do you feel?

You must mentally walk yourself through the experience of attaining your goals and visualizing success on the other side. Those visualizations will get you through middle-of-the-night doubts when you think, *I can't.*

Push yourself in your level of thinking. Take the time to break your goals down to get that visualization. Half of putting the work in getting from where you are to point A (figuratively stating) is visualization because it ties everything together. When I have that level of visualization in my mind and realize it's possible, my mind will execute and say, *Okay, now I can achieve that!* Further, I'm willing to do the steps of listening to this podcast, reading this book, and surrounding myself with the right people to help me with whatever I'm trying to accomplish. When you visualize something, it can give you the same feeling as when you achieve it. Visualization can give you a taste of how sweet the future could be.

Still, some people will visualize and stay in the visualization. They trick themselves into believing they don't have to accomplish their goals, but action is vital! Guard yourself by not giving yourself a pass based on visualization. When you visualize, you let it change your mindset. Then, start planning the intentional things you're going to feed your mind, and you put the plan into action. Finally, you begin.

Growing your mind is lifelong. For example, I've had the dream and vision to write this book since I was twenty-eight. Yet, I put it off for twenty-two years. Then, in 2012, I had my first seizure, and the emergency-room doctor told me that I had metastatic brain cancer and gave me six months to live. I thought… *This is it! I had all these things I wanted to accomplish, but the runway is over.* Before that diagnosis, I always thought I had plenty of time to achieve certain things. I was forty-three, and I thought I had a long runway ahead of me and had plenty of time. I had no sense of urgency. But mortality smacked me in the face. That was a wall of frustration for me. I felt disgusted with myself for wasting time and wasting my God-given abilities.

Though the diagnosis stunned me, it gave me a sense of urgency. I still had the desire to write the book and the need to accomplish *so* much more. At that point, I had to remember one piece of information—I needed to switch from the subconscious to the conscious. I couldn't allow random thoughts to enter my mind; I had to develop a plan and be intentional about what went into my mind. Thankfully, I have a rule: beat yourself up for twenty-four hours and try to figure out how to move forward for tomorrow. So, the next day, I woke up and said,

"Regardless of the outcome, this is going to be the most productive six months of my life." I realized that if I was going to achieve my goals, I had to do it now. Getting a second opinion was the first item on my to-do list. I went to a different physician, who gave me a different outlook and offered some hope through surgery. After getting the tumor removed, my life was no longer at risk, but I faced more obstacles that I will share with you as we move forward.

Frustrations are specific to each person. My first debilitating frustration occurred when I recognized I could do much more than what I was doing. As a kid, I had a vision for my life, of what I could be and what I would accomplish. As I grew up, I began losing hope, which happens to many people. How could you achieve a vision without hope? Fear then convinced me that success would be too hard, and the steps to attain it were too long. Still, based on my childhood goals, I knew I wasn't where I wanted to be. Every day that frustration got me to the point where when I heard that nugget of information from the speaker at that sales meeting, the lightbulb went off. Everyone has to look for that lightbulb moment. Ask yourself, "Am I really frustrated? Am I really at the point where enough is enough?"

I encourage you not to let facing death be what creates your haste to act. Learn from my experience; don't get to where, because of your lack of action, your urgency is so great that there isn't enough time to fit in everything you desire. We all start with enough time to achieve our desires. But if we aren't intentional, we procrastinate until it gets to a point of urgency or elimination. Can you stop this cycle before it begins? Though the tumor was removed, it can always regrow, so I have to get it checked every six months. Every six months, I face my mortality. Most people without health issues can't understand my anxiety level. I must deal with the thoughts of, *Did it regrow?* or *Did it stay static?* I must get an MRI regularly, send it to the doctor, and wait three days. During that time, I'm thinking, *What happened? What about my kids? What am I going to do? What about my businesses?* All these thoughts run through my head. Again, I urge you to learn this valuable lesson early: you're not promised tomorrow—the time is now!

If you act with urgency, you will see results. Most people will not have the diagnosis I faced at age forty-three. Most people aren't forced to live with the same sense of urgency I was. Sadly, you may wake up at eighty years old with no more runway because you kept saying, "Tomorrow, the next day, when the summer comes, when the kids go back to school, in the new year..." and, before you knew it, all of those years passed by and you never achieved your goals. Remember, the time is always now!

Besides death, the only thing that can stop you from taking action, regardless of your age or circumstances, is giving up.

There's simply no cure for quitting.

And there's no cure for someone who has declared they don't have more time when they do. Even though not everything you will face has answers, you can't give up. You can throw yourself a pity party for twenty-four hours, but the next morning, figure out a way forward because if you give up, you're done. When you say, "This is it for me," and you've resigned yourself to that fact, it's over because no one can change your attitude. Only you can... if you never quit! If you're reading this book, I know you haven't given up!

When you're still reaching for another answer, you haven't quit. You're not done if you're still buying books, spending money, reading motivational quotes and articles, or asking people for more information.

You may throw yourself a pity party, but you haven't quit. The person who has genuinely given up is not buying this book or doing anything. They're done! Some might say, "I'm done, but I'm going to read this one more book." That person's real message is: "I don't want to tell you I'm still moving forward in case I fail. I don't want you in on the secret, but I will try this one more thing." In their mind, they're really hitting that wall of frustration. They're saying, "I know there's more—that's why I'm willing to put in the effort to read this book."

To break the frustration wall, you must take action and move forward. Unfortunately, most people do the same things over and over. They just can't figure life out, which goes back to the subconscious. The subconscious makes you think that the world is out to get you, while the conscious says, "I keep feeding my mind unintentionally by consuming the world as it comes to me." Statistics prove that this is how most people approach life. They don't feed their minds or grow their thinking intentionally based on their goals. However, that is precisely what will bring you to the next level. You must start feeding your mind with things that will retrain your thinking. Watching professional sports and seeing an athlete execute a play is based on something the person fed his or her mind and practiced. The subconscious reacted based on something the athlete did to intentionally train the brain.

It takes most people hitting a wall of frustration once or multiple times before they realize they need to retrain their thinking. Can you retrain your thinking without hitting a wall of frustration? Absolutely. Most people try to learn from their mistakes, but the goal in life is to shorten the runway to change. Very self-aware people go down the road of success and say, "I made that mistake; let me evaluate it." That approach is good. However, the super successful say, "I don't have to learn from my mistakes. I can find an experienced, trusted advisor and ask them about the mistakes they have learned from and the lessons they learned and apply those to my life."

The reason I wrote this book is to give others a blueprint. I want to explain to others how my mistakes transformed me. I want you, as a reader, to take my experiences and say, "I don't have to make the same mistakes that Brett did," so that you can go farther, faster. You can decide to be intentional, grow your thinking, and improve your decision-making, which will change your life.

If you allow the subconscious to control your decisions, you will be driven by the here and now. You will be driven without information based on how to accomplish what you're doing successfully. If you're growing your thinking and being intentional in your thoughts, your thinking will be driven based on purposeful information that you put in your mind from other experts and people who have had success. Your decisions will be driven based on a subset of information from other successful drivers of thought. You want to grow your thinking to where you can process decisions more intelligently or productively because of the information you've placed in your mind.

We must produce better results in defined areas we're trying to accomplish based on where we are and want to be. One-size thinking doesn't fit all. When growing your thinking, you must do it daily and as soon as you get up. When you wake up in the morning, you get to decide what kind of morning you will have. If you say, "Today is going to be a bad day," it will be a bad day. Can you have a bad thing happen in the morning? Sure! But there are two ways to look at it. An intentional thinker says, "I'm not going to let this ruin the rest of my day," and moves on.

Intentional thinking challenges you to find a solution to make things work so that you can find a way forward. Don't focus on the one reason that something doesn't work. Find the reasons that it will. To become intentional, you must fight the mind's desire to be complacent. Fight the urge to give yourself a pass to quit before you start. Anybody can critique what I'm writing and try to find a way that it will not work, which all goes into a naysayer's way of thinking. There are a hundred thousand reasons not to start today—and zero excuses.

PRACTICAL STEPS FORWARD

1. First, decide to reevaluate your thinking. You must realize that you subconsciously consume the world with no plan.

2. Second, you must create a vision statement of the areas that will help you become who you want to be and what you want to accomplish. Figure out the areas of the plan and ask yourself what you want to improve in those areas. That's the vision statement you will use in your visualization exercises.

3. Third, to execute the plan, you must plan intentionally to feed your mind, whether it's a podcast, a book, or a wise counsel around you.

4. Finally, start. You must act from when you wake up to when you sleep daily.

STEP THREE
REFRAME YOUR ATTITUDE

The lowest of low doesn't have to be so.

Attitude is a choice.

> Your attitude is not the result of what you feel; it is the result of how you decide to act.

Bad days are inevitable; the unforeseen happens; we think life is unfair; an unexpected loss will occur. Surviving a brain tumor and an airplane crash (we'll get to that later) has taught me that pain does not take away my ability or responsibility to choose.

> Although experiences can seem overwhelmingly painful, it's what they teach us and how we respond that truly matters.

I've discovered how to remain consistent and determined with my positive attitude even when things are outside my control. Daily decisions regarding your attitude decide whether you create a progressive solution or remain part of the problem.

Boundaryless Success focuses on intentional choices rather than subconscious chances. An inconsistent attitude will lead to unpredictable results. Everyone will fluctuate between good and bad choices. I challenge you to choose your attitude and remain consistent in your commitment.

Just because you fell off doesn't mean you cannot get back on track. Are you ready to learn how to reframe your attitude and shift your life from *I wish* to *I did* to *look where I'm headed*?

LET'S TAKE THE NEXT STEPS TOWARD BOUNDARYLESS SUCCESS

- What is attitude? How do you approach problems? How do you move forward? When you are a child, everything is a possibility. Learn how to pull a lesson out of every experience. Look for the lessons and opportunities daily.
- Intentionally focus on the positive outcome you desire.
- Ask yourself every day, "What am I capable of doing?"
- Have an honest moment with yourself.
- List the opportunities.

ATTITUDE IS A CHOICE

Have you had something come up that you didn't expect? A party, schedule changes, an accident, etc.? Did it conflict with something else that you had intended to do? Did it affect your attitude? Did you find yourself after it was over saying, "I knew that was going to happen?" What about a time when you were somewhere, and the opposite happened? Have you ever thought about why? Is it possible that how you approached it, your attitude and your thought process affected the outcome? What if you approached it with an attitude of "No matter why this happened, what can I learn from the experience?" rather than seeing it as a nuisance? If you think about the opposing experiences, your attitude was at play in the outcome. We have been talking about being intentional—this is a hidden secret of people who succeed in their personal and professional lives and their ability to choose their attitude. Start by writing down the things that affect your attitude. Write down ways to take a positive rather than a negative approach. When you first begin this, it will have to be a daily occurrence, and you'll experience the progress. As you see the wins, it'll become easier to reframe. However, never let up because, just like a diet, if you quit, the progress retracts.

Attitude is a choice. I would go further to say that attitude is a daily choice. No one, no place, or thing is responsible for your attitude except you. Most people know and perhaps even understand this; that's not the issue. The challenge is that knowing and understanding don't equate to implementing and doing. As a mentor, I have observed that a poor attitude is the most common impediment to success. I get to know individuals through one-on-one meetings, and they open up about their dreams and ambitions. Often, they also share their obstacles to achieving them. I can genuinely hear my mentee's passion and desire to achieve big things while they share their fear, self-doubt, and lack of confidence. They allow these negative feelings to shape their attitude rather than focusing on their talents and abilities, resulting in an undesirable outcome—or at least less than they had envisioned. Boundaryless Success will never be reached without the right attitude.

Let's recall, *attitude is a choice.* Your attitude will either work for you or against you. What would that look like if your attitude told the story of your life beginning today and going backward? Would you be proud of it? Would you want to share it with your family and friends? Contemplate those answers as we continue.

I understand the importance of attitude from both a personal and professional standpoint. Personally, my goals have become the victim of my negative attitude. They've suffered to become a reality because of my negative mindset. I had many hopes, dreams, and aspirations when I was younger. I read magazines and business journals, envisioning myself as a successful leader. I could clearly see how I would lead, what I would say, and the impact I would make. Even with a vivid imagination about my future, my self-esteem and attitude kept me from believing that someone like me could achieve it. I allowed my negative thinking to determine what I did, what I said, and how I responded in life. My perspective toward life formed a negative mental attitude. It was as though there were two of me in my head. One cheered me on and told me, *You can do this*. The other discouraged me and warned me against taking the risk. I felt torn between two inner voices. Yet still, I could make a choice. I didn't understand how to choose between what I wanted and what I felt.

Fast-forward to my adult life. I knew I had talent when I started my career, yet I got fired three times. If you were to assess your attitude as an employee of yourself, how would it rank? What improvement would you suggest for yourself? Would you be a star performer at the bottom or someone with tremendous potential that seemed like a wasted talent? I started my working career constantly allowing self-doubt to enter my life, although I had had some modest success. Have you ever had times of success only to marginalize it when you get around others who are also successful? You see someone who appears to be a better father, mother, friend, or employee? Again, you must constantly guard yourself against the comparison trap. Our intentionality keeps us from going against the natural negative tendencies that make us think *I can't* versus *I can*. Take a moment to think about what you are struggling with so that we can focus together on how choosing the attitude with which you face the struggle will assist you in getting further faster. With those fresh on your mind, let's walk together to reframe your perspective.

Even as a young adult, I struggled with my confidence for years. My low opinion of myself resulted from negative self-talk. I wanted to measure up and be what I thought the perfect salesperson should be. Things shifted for me when I focused on growth materials about self-image. From that point, I constantly attended growth seminars. I was hungry to realize my potential. Exposing myself to teaching and mentoring empowered me to take an attitude assessment. The assessment forced me to look at all the *I can'ts* that prevented me from confidently pursuing my goals. That was the moment it clicked: attitude is a choice. Once I understood I controlled my attitude, I intentionally worked on my self-talk. I'm talking about daily, hourly, and minute-by-minute. I worked on retraining my brain to think in alignment with what I wanted in life. While this seems like an intense process (and it is), this attitude became natural with consistency. Although you will still experience ups and downs, the thinking that you will have allows you to navigate your issues positively. Don't lose hope; you will have challenges when you reframe poor thinking, but your attitude toward these will enable you to move forward successfully.

I recall once being challenged by the VP of Sales; he called me into the hall and said, "Son, you've got more talent than anyone else. When will you do something with it and stop wasting it?" He challenged me to grow my mind through reading and to write down specific goals and things I wanted to accomplish. Let's be candid—this comment initially aggravated me at the time. I was upset with him for his words and how they made me feel. I thought, *Who does he think he is? Doesn't he know how hard I've worked to be here? Does he know how much I have overcome to be doing what I am doing?* Let me ask you a question: have you ever heard something good for you but struggled to receive it because you took offense? That is exactly what I felt at that moment.

> Whatever you're thinking, the reality is probably the opposite.

I overcame his statement by remembering these words. You see, I thought what he said was him sharing something that was speaking against me, but the fact was that he was sharing something to motivate me to move forward.

Realizing that his words were not meant to be taken as an insult, I followed the instructions, specifically wrote down my goals, and started creating a plan. From that point, my plan skyrocketed, but much trench work went on before then. I had to get serious about doing the inner work to realize what I wanted to be and stop wasting my time.

Do you see how your attitude can limit or advance you? You must decide to shift your focus and control the thoughts coming into your mind rather than allowing the negative thoughts to control your thinking. *If you choose not to be intentional with your attitude, then your attitude can and will work against your personal and professional goals.*

REFRAMING YOUR ATTITUDE

Attitudes are subconsciously formed based on life experiences, shaping your thought processes. Those thoughts, in turn, play a prominent role in your self-esteem. The only way to reverse this process is by intentionally choosing your attitude daily. Reframing your mindset first began when we started repairing your self-esteem. Once you have begun, this will allow you to be self-aware enough to recognize the need for intentional thinking. By allowing your mind to be cluttered with negative or self-defeating thoughts like, *people like me can't do that*, or *I'll never be good enough to do that*, it becomes impossible to change the narrative you have written about yourself. Self-esteem opens the door to change what you think about yourself. However, this is just the beginning.

From the professional standpoint of serving as a leader and mentor, I've witnessed competent individuals struggle with producing desired success and outcomes due to their negative attitudes. As a leader in the sales industry, I need to get to know the people I work alongside. Knowing an employee's goals, dreams, and struggles helps the company succeed and move forward together. In getting to know these people, I learned about their goals, dreams, and aspirations. My company culture promotes a shared sense of success, so I pride myself on mentoring and sharing advice with those seeking it. I've observed a pattern through my hundreds of conversations. It is the disconnect between what people express they desire and what they actively pursue. Witnessing this disconnect has given me insight into the importance of attitude in chasing success. Now, walk with me as we take the next step in reframing your perspective.

BECOMING AN INTENTIONAL THINKER

Becoming intentional in your thinking involves directing your thoughts rather than letting your thoughts direct you. Have you ever thought about that? How often do you go through the motions aimlessly without direction as to why or what the result will be? Some part of yourself fuels your thoughts, whether or not you know it. The subconscious mind works off of your last failure to influence your decisions. It holds onto experiences and uses the good, bad, and indifferent details to become the basis of your thoughts. As children, we are excited to learn and explore, unaware of any rational or irrational dangers. However, we have been conditioned based on our experiences and have drawn on them as we've matured. Intentional thinking requires us to revert to infancy concerning what's possible, utilizing our experiences and applying our lessons to create our deliberate thought.

POSITIVE SELF-TALK IS THE KEY TO CHOOSING WISELY WITH YOUR ATTITUDE

You will have an attitude, whether or not you are motivated. It's going to be a positive or negative one. But we can control our minds to say somewhere in there, "I need to make a change. I know I'm capable of more, whether personal or professional." In my journey, I knew there was something I could do differently, so I began evaluating each circumstance that led me to that point. I recall going to church one time. I had a lot of negative things going on in my life, including alcoholism, personal relationship struggles, and other self-inflicted hardships. I listened to the sermon, and the pastor talked about how we can do all these things more positively and impactfully. I left with the determination that I would change those things, but I still had the same low self-esteem and a lack of visualization. After a week, I had the same circle of influence that I brought back into my life that was actuating those thoughts and negativity. I still thought negatively about my situation and what I could accomplish and achieve. The pastor was pouring in the talk, which at the moment, motivated me, but as soon as I left service, I returned to my old way of thinking and attitude.

Many people are in that boat. They hear something great, but they're left alone when that person's voice is removed. What you say to yourself is more important than anything anyone can say. Choose a positive self-image and attitude. When doing those things, you're talking to yourself rather than some outside source. When you listen to the motivational stuff or read this book to boost yourself, it's building on your foundation. To me, motivation is like the addict or the alcoholic and the fix. You drink ten beers or hit the drug of your choice, and you get that high. But when it wears off, you double up. The same happens when you try to jump and hear that motivational person. You go down further than you were because, for a moment, you thought of what was possible. Then the subconscious forces talk to you because you're not talking to yourself and creating what's possible. Stop it! Feed your brain intentional positive self-talk daily, nonstop.

Where would I be today if I had let my attitude take over after my brain tumor diagnosis? Do you see the critical role attitude played in my outcome? Despite a challenging situation, I decided what to think and how to respond. Imagine if I had just accepted the emergency-room doctor at face value and withered away in self-pity for the next six months. I honestly believe that, in my case, I would have died. Not because I had to but because I would have given up the will to live based on one person's opinion. Even today, medical professionals learn that a patient's attitude is as essential as the treatment plan. No matter what you face in life, you have to intentionally visualize what success looks like, put in a plan of action, and work toward it daily. While recovering from my surgery, I repeatedly listened to motivational speakers, pastors, and books on tape about self-help because I had already chosen to take control of my attitude.

SUCCESS IS FOUND IN YOUR DAILY ROUTINE

How would you sum up your daily routine? Does it drive your attitude, or does your attitude drive it? How important do you think your daily routine relates to your mindset? What things do you identify with immediately that you would change or implement to retrain your brain? Whatever you focus on is what you get. Aristotle said, "You are what you do repeatedly," and I like to say this,

> "Success is the direct result of your habits."

People who achieve Boundaryless Success work toward it daily.

> We cannot have a desired destination and be unwilling to get there.

Our daily routine or habits allow us to get from having a goal to accomplishing one.

I've heard a lot of reasons why people struggle with implementing and sticking to a daily routine. For some, it works against their instinct; for others, it seems impossible due to their lifestyles. I, too, face challenges with my daily routine. Because of my brain tumor, some lasting effects impact my daily physical abilities. Some days, I feel fully mobile, capable, and vibrant. On other days, I may struggle to move my hand or arm or suffer a seizure that requires an impromptu rest time to recover. This is why I am so heavy on the importance of attitude. Yes, I can see the opportunity to become discouraged, frustrated, or upset some days. But when I intentionally think about it, what would that do to accomplish my goals or change my situation? Nothing. This is why even on the hardest days of my life, I still maintain my commitments to my daily routine, even if it sometimes requires a few adjustments. Walking through my healing process, I have developed an attitude that views setbacks as setups. I choose to see the opportunity in the challenge. On days I cannot use my hand as planned, I'll use my voice and record what I want to write. And when I need to rest and recover during a time I had planned to do something else, I work to reschedule or delegate to ensure things get done. You can develop a plan to adjust that works for your circumstances and with your resources.

Everyone is different; some people are naturally inclined to a regimented lifestyle, while others are not. You need a goal and plan for achievement every day. You need somewhere to go back and benchmark that you accomplished those things. If only it was as easy as taking a pill to fix everything and make us perfect in these areas. By intentionally reprogramming your mind, you create a life that allows you to transition from downhill to uphill. The choice is yours alone.

PRACTICAL STEPS FORWARD

1. First, acknowledge and embrace that your attitude is your choice.
2. Second, you must commit to practicing healthy self-talk by intentionally choosing what you feed your brain.
3. Third, limit exposure by taking control of what you think and not allowing circumstances to cause you to spiral.
4. Finally, take responsibility for your attitude, envision where you want to be, and intentionally use daily actions to get there.

STEP FOUR
ENVISION DESIRED CHANGE

Vision will always reveal the way forward.

Where do you see yourself in five years?

Have you invested the time to think of your life in the future?

The two questions I just posed are prevalent in conversations regarding dreams, goals, and success. Would it surprise you to know that most people struggle to answer them? As shocking as it may seem, the average person doesn't have a clear response regarding their aspirations for the future.

> The gut-wrenching truth is that many individuals desire to escape their reality but have no clear vision of how to get there.

Change must be envisioned before it is experienced; otherwise, you are doomed to repeat what you see, whether or not you like it. I know the last sentence was a bit of a tongue-twister, but please do not miss the point of the statement. Have you ever thought, *Gosh, I want so much more out of life*? While this is a genuine thought generated from a sincere desire, let's get real—what does *more* actually look like when unsupported by a noun? The word *more* was created to work in conjunction with a noun.

So, just wanting more in life alone is not enough to produce more. You must envision the specific change you desire in order to take actionable steps toward experiencing it.

The two leading questions I shared at the start of this step are asked to stimulate a mental picture of what you look at when you see yourself operating in your strength zone. In Step Six, we will fully explore this concept, but for this step, consider your strength zone as operating at capacity within your talent and abilities. The mental picture is what the desired change looks and feels like on every level—mind, body, soul, and spirit. Are you following me?

Now, using this definition, let's explore those questions and a few others. Where do you see yourself in five years? Are you currently on the pathway to hit that mark? When was the last time you measured your progress? What do you need to tweak for achievement? And have you invested the time to think of your life in the future? The mental picture you see or don't see in response to the questions will fall into pain, necessity, or purpose categories. A pain picture is an event that actually happened, a necessity picture is the result of unresolved pain, and a purpose picture is an aspiration.

> Pain and purpose can shape who you are, who you are becoming, and what you accomplish in life. The one you value most will define how you view life and its possibility.

I said the one you value most. You may think, *Who would value pain?* Most people who value pain do so unintentionally and live unaware until it interrupts some area of their life that they value enough to investigate why. You value pain by holding onto painful memories, experiences, or situations and using it to drive what you do or do not do. This can occur at both the conscious and subconscious levels of our thinking. For example, you may remember how terrible it felt when you applied, prepared for, and interviewed for a job you did not get. Then you use this memory as why you stay at a job or a career you hate. Consciously when this happens, refraining from repeating the pain seems wise. But, it is actually unwise in this case because all you do is run away from what you want because you allowed the memory of the pain to become bigger than your vision for the future. Take it from someone who has allowed the pain to become a *why* in the past,

> It is dangerous to your future to allow pain to be the center of your *why*.

See, when it comes to pain, it is only concerned with the moment, whereas purpose is focused on the future. Purpose cultivates an internal commitment to an unseen future that you are fully confident is possible. With this commitment, the resilience to endure rejection, failure, or any other emotion generated from pain manifests through action and consistency. Purpose strengthens you to attain success. Getting back to the thought-provoking questions we've been considering, they can help shape a mental picture that can inspire hope or dread. Some say, "A man without a vision is a man without a future. A man without a future will always return to his past." Boundaryless Success principles empower you to access your envisioned future, but it all begins with your vision. When I grasped this principle, my mental picture changed the trajectory of my life. Once I got beyond Steps One, Two, and Three in my personal life and began developing a vision, I was ready to take big steps toward the future I had always envisioned.

The vision I imagined for my life was something no one I knew at the time had experienced. My life was surrounded by hardworking people who didn't make it beyond the middle class. I saw some of the best people you could ever know struggle to make ends meet. While I admired them for their work ethic and character in many ways, I envisioned a future that would lead to more opportunities with my life and talents.

I was convinced I could become someone great and influential worldwide. I grew up listening to success principles. I knew and remembered them, they motivated me, and I believed they would lead to something significant in my life. I wanted to become a leader of a top-performing sales organization that created hundreds of jobs. I dreamed of leading, training, and motivating thousands to achieve Boundaryless Success. Imagine someone like me—from humble beginnings, no formal education, and with little personal success—with a massive vision like that. As audacious and unlikely as it sounds, I held onto it. I wasn't 100 percent sure how to get there, but I was determined to achieve this mental picture. Even though it might appear that I had a great distance to get there, the key was understanding where I wanted to be and what it would require.

One compelling point about vision is that it will reveal the way forward. Think about that statement,

Vision will reveal the way forward.

Understanding that concept is vital to this journey. Vision takes you from where you are to where you want to be. It is your guide to achieving dreams, goals, and ambitions. But here is another thought: if your vision reveals the way forward, then the absence of vision will... do what? I would dare say leave you stuck or stagnant—not progressing beyond your current position in life. This is why you must envision the change you desire.

Until now, we've been walking through Steps One through Three and realizing the importance of acting on a plan. But, in that plan, we also must have a specific picture of what success looks like. Envisioning success is critical to reaching it. The image expresses what success looks like and how you will feel about attaining it in that area. Step Four will serve as a springboard toward your desired future.

Let's begin the next leg of our journey by breaking down how to envision your desired change.

UNDERSTANDING THE MENTAL PICTURE

To paint your desired mental picture, you must understand the meaning and purpose of the three primary pictures: pain, necessity, and purpose. To clarify the concept of mental pictures, I will transparently share my journey with weight loss and how I used this process to reach success.

I am a fifty-three-year-old man who has struggled with my weight since I was eleven. Yep, that is four whole decades. There was a time that I would have never shared this part of my life because of shame and embarrassment. For so long, I allowed my pain picture to limit how I saw myself and interacted with others.

Pain Picture: This is a mental snapshot of one or more low points in life. Pain pictures work as an emotional boundary to avoid experiencing repeated pain. This picture is a self-protecting mechanism that can hinder future success.

My struggles with weight loss contributed to my low self-esteem. I've shared in previous steps that I always knew I could achieve success. Still, considering my humble living conditions, I struggled to pursue it confidently. The perception of where I came from subdued my determination to take action toward my dreams. Problems with my self-esteem led to me finding comfort in eating more than was necessary for one day. I would eat, and eat, and eat, all in hopes of ultimately feeling better. The temporary high from eating enabled me to ignore the long-term effect of overeating on my body and self-esteem. Before I realized it, I had a serious issue with my weight. So from one low self-esteem moment to another, I would get motivated to lose weight and sooner or later be back in the same rut with food and nowhere close to my fitness goal. This persisted throughout my teenage years, early twenties, thirties, and mid-forties. Eventually, my oncologist told me that reducing my sugar intake and incorporating a healthy diet would significantly reduce the chance of my tumor growing. After countless starts and restarts, my life and health had gotten to where I might lose my life if I did not make a permanent change. Weight loss went from a pain picture to a necessity picture with a life-threatening diagnosis, and only then could I make real changes.

Necessity Picture: This is a picture created from unresolved pain. Necessity pictures often inspire action and drive execution because of the potential consequences attached to the picture. What the weight of a pain picture cannot produce alone can join forces with a necessity picture to motivate you into action.

For me, my health scare became the necessity picture. I feared the negative prognosis given by my treating doctors. As reality kicked in, I realized I wanted to live long and healthily.

> I didn't want to allow the pain of my past to cut off the potential of my future.

Instinctively, something shifted inside of me. A determination to live healthily became my focus. And so, after over fourteen thousand plus days of struggling to overcome weight-loss struggles, my health goals materialized. In the past, I felt like I couldn't control my urge to eat, but something shifted. I became disciplined. After reading many books and joining a dozen or more fitness clubs and plans, I finally submitted to the wisdom of my dietician and personal trainer and succeeded with the prescribed health plan. Soon, I was feeling, looking, and living a healthy life in a little over six months. Imagine that? I went from being an overweight forty-something-year-old man struggling for four decades to live a healthy lifestyle to a man who defied the medical odds and is actively living a vibrant, healthy lifestyle.

So what changed in less than a year? I'll tell you the answer: my mental picture changed. The fulfillment I once received from overeating was no longer worth it. Listen, I have lived, coached, and taught hundreds of people on this one life-transforming principle:

> No one makes a decision until the pain has gotten greater than the ability to operate without it.

That was precisely what happened to me with my weight-loss challenges and health scare.

> When you decide that the pain is worse than the work needed to make the gain, the need for change will be something you embrace, not avoid.

In my situation, I stopped viewing my life as the poor little eleven-year-old who didn't come from the right side of the tracks and relied on food to feel good. I had to let go of that pain picture! My health scare forced me to grow up mentally and emotionally. Maturing mentally and emotionally enabled me to envision living a life where I was healthy, fit, full of energy, present with my family, leading my businesses, and living as long as possible. Yes, the necessity picture gave me the ultimatum of *get fit or die young*, but ultimately, I had to decide and take charge to experience change. It is important to note that not every necessity picture has a positive outcome. Some people get to this point where life demands a change or else, but they do not take action. Many die, lose their families, destroy their businesses and credit, or worse, all because they didn't pursue their purpose picture.

Purpose Picture: This is an authentic moment with yourself where you stop blaming others and inventing excuses. A purpose picture directly results from self-awareness. It is what gets and keeps you going, motivates hard work, and promotes resiliency.

This is why I encourage you not to wait on a necessity picture. If you are reading this book, the time is now to work toward your purpose picture. I get that my story sounds like the storybook ending, but it will not be the same for everyone. For some, the necessity picture may become apparent when it is too late. You can use your current pain picture to discover your purpose picture.

The purpose picture leads to self-realization and the fulfillment of one's potential. The *Purpose Driven* book series offers a widely popular message on discovering your purpose in multiple areas of life. Author Pastor Rick Warren taps into the heart and soul of a subject that people spend a lifetime attempting to understand, "What is my purpose?"

> Purpose brings a sense of meaning and value to individuals who unearth it.

Pastor Rick famously shared in the *Purpose Driven Life*, "In living for your purposes, you'll find meaning in every moment of your life." I was able to experience the reviving power of purpose after my health scare. I went from being a man who lived to eat to a man who ate to live. Do you see the difference in my mental picture about food? The entire time I struggled with overeating, I did not view food from a purpose picture perspective. I considered it from a pain-picture perspective. Having no purpose, I allowed food to become something it wasn't created to be—my comforter. But when I was forced through the necessity picture to take an introspective look at my life, where I was headed, and where I wanted to be, the fog of pain cleared my mental image. It allowed me to finally receive and appreciate the purpose of food. That may sound ridiculously elementary at my age. Yet, as a forty-something-year-old man, I had to learn the authentic purpose of food to change my relationship with it.

One thing I want to warn you of is that humility is required to genuinely discover your purpose.

> You will not clearly see your purpose if you allow pride or shame to distort your vision through denial.

A decision must be made—either you want the product of pain, or you want purpose in your life. This requires honesty about the seen and unseen things in your life. Unseen struggles contribute to the majority of seen failures.

> We cannot hide our real problems and expect lasting change.

Think back over my story. A great deal of what led to my weight-loss challenges were unseen problems that only I knew about. Whether or not I acknowledged it, I knew the how and why behind my overeating and weight-loss challenges. Yet, I refused to deal with them at the root. Refusing to be straight up with myself caused me to remain stuck in place and nearly caused me an early death. Learn from my mistakes. Don't be afraid to face what's really going on. To help you, I am sharing two ways to discover your purpose picture, starting today:

- **Failure:** It will teach you how much you can do! I view failure as a unique insight into growing my talents and abilities. This perception has made failure a trusted tool in my success chest.

> Borrow from the experience of others rather than having to wait on pain.

- **Evaluation:** Do this often and consistently. Evaluation enables you to measure your progress and implement necessary changes for success. Do not wait until you struggle or fail to evaluate. Build it into your ongoing plan, and it eliminates pain.

Most people have some idea of their purpose but let go of it because of low self-esteem, hope, and lack of execution. Having a strategy will help you get clear again and truly see your purpose detached from pain.

PAINT THE PICTURE

In life, experiences create memories. Some experiences become a part of our long-term memory, and others impact us at specific moments in life. Our take on how we experience and remember life makes us unique. We purposefully hold so many life-changing feelings near and dear to our hearts, such as how we felt at the birth of a child, our first love, the day we got married, details of going on vacation, and other happy events. There are also embarrassing or painful memories we hold on to, like the shame of failure, being laughed at or ridiculed in school, getting fired for the first time, or the agony of losing a loved one. These memories work together to create the pictures that contribute to who we become or limit what we achieve. You can use both the good and bad in life to paint your purpose picture.

Before I elaborate on how to paint your picture, let me show their power. I once knew a man whose mother left him with her parents shortly after giving birth because he was the product of an affair. One can only imagine the potential rejection, confusion, and hurt he grew through from his childhood until adulthood. Yet, he's become a wonderful husband and loving father despite the treatment of his birth parents. How is that possible after being abandoned by his birth mother? Shouldn't he be destined for an emotionally disconnected life due to the absence of nurturing and acceptance from his birth mother? Some might nod, and others shake their heads. Our Yes's and No's are opinions concerning what this young man or others like him can do. I know fully that there are mounds of valid research on reasons for success or failure in life after the rejection of a birth parent. Yet, individuals like this young man with similar obstacles still defy the odds. In his case, he became what he wanted to be, not allowing his birth mother's statistics or unanswered questions to hold his purpose hostage. At some point, he decided what he wanted his life and family to look like, which he pursued and ultimately achieved.

The story above demonstrates how your mental picture can impact your outcome. Painting the picture sounds like an artsy expression, but it means to implement, execute, or manifest your purpose through consistent unrelenting action. When creating the image of what you want to achieve, begin by painting that picture in your head. Then, start working to create what you envision in your mind. Many people who have grown up in unfortunate circumstances allow pain to fuel their actions, which leads to the creation of unhealthy cycles. The difference between repeating pain and making a different decision manifests from what you see inside your mental picture of the future.

Painting the picture is learning to become intentional about the decisions that you're making. If I go back through all the steps, when I get to the picture part, I've reached the point where the pain has become unbearable. Then, I'm deciding to change. That is the power of choice. You must take responsibility to change. Blaming everyone else solves nothing and causes you to regress.

> The truth is, where you are right now is the sum of every decision you have ever made.

Many decisions are unintentional; they are simply the result of an emotion. But to tap into this book's value, you must reach a point where you are ready to change, stop making excuses, and intentionally paint the purpose you see and desire. You can paint your purpose picture no matter what you've gone through. I have defined three simple steps to help you create a mental image reflecting what you want from your life.

PRACTICAL STEPS FORWARD

1. Become self-aware: You must be conscious of what is fueling your mental picture. You are responsible for knowing the drive behind what you do or don't do. This understanding empowers you to understand your strengths and weaknesses and expose potential threats from within that may affect future success.
2. Evaluate: Your mental picture either serves your purpose or perpetuates your pain. Evaluate to find your way forward.
3. Decide what you want to see: Take ownership of your dreams, goals, and ambitions by defining what you want to see in your life, career, or family. You cannot live life on autopilot and become disappointed by where you end up. Boundaryless Success is the result of intentional thinking and mindful actions in life.

STEP FIVE

EVALUATE YOUR INTERNAL WORLD

The simplest things are easy to understand…
but they're the most difficult to do daily.

What does evaluating your internal world mean? Have you ever looked inside to see what honestly drives you without bias? Have you attempted to see yourself the way others see you without making excuses or combating their evaluation? Do you even have someone that you trust enough to give you a positive assessment without you calling it criticism?

> Understand that the people that care about you the most are the ones that tell you what you need to hear, not what you want to hear.

Evaluating reoccurring patterns and themes that result from identifying unresolved internal struggles can break ineffective habits and shift the entire course of your life. I firmly believe through personal experience that the way to change unsuccessful cycles is discovered through a 360-degree internal walk-around. This will be achieved by getting inside our thoughts and seeing what's driving our decisions. I will list examples, thought-provoking questions, and processes for you to do your 360-degree walk-around. This can be exciting; however, it will be hard work. When I did this myself, it took me many hours of staring at the wall, coming to terms with myself, and realizing that I controlled my destiny through my thoughts.

I have faith in you. Do you have faith in yourself? I recall hearing this statement many years ago, "Get out of your own way." It made sense, but it was a thought-starter that didn't lead me to change my life. Understand that as you read through the text of this book, many of the thoughts, concepts, and steps will be thought-starters for you until you repetitively review and apply them as a permanent part of how you think. Even though I said I didn't understand, I continued to come to the same frustration when I would have some success that would soon falter and leave me wondering why. I would look at every angle and figure out why the progress stopped until one day, EUREKA! I finally realized that it was not anybody else's fault but mine. "It's you, Brett! Get out of your own way." Have you had a familiar frustrating experience? Has someone ever told you something that sounded simple, but you struggled to apply it? Right now, I can imagine you with a smirk, a twinkle in your eye, and a desire to shout for joy. This step will equip you with how to get out of your own way—tools to empower yourself. So, pull your pen and paper out, and let's roll!

PREPARING FOR AN INTERNAL WALK-AROUND

The road to Boundaryless Success starts with you. Just think about that statement for a second. What comes to your mind when you hear it? How does that make you feel? Are you ready to do something about that feeling?

I hope that your response to the last question is YES! Because you are the only reason you have not accomplished the level of success you can attain. Now, I don't intend to be harsh or critical but think about that last statement. The good news is that you have the opportunity to break that cycle because everyone can reach their highest potential.

> How many intrusive, negative, and self-sabotaging thoughts have stolen your courage, faith, and resilience to attain goals?

I need you to understand that those thoughts reflect something going on inside you. As we covered in Step One, those feelings of inferiority came from a place of low self-esteem, and you must work to fix it. Hopefully, you are at a comfortable place in your self-esteem now. Some people fear that if they stick their necks out and fail, they'll be embarrassed. They will be in a situation where they will be on public display at a low moment. But I'm here to tell you… you will fail if you think that way.

> We experience 99 percent of what we believe.

Instead, choose to forgive yourself upfront because failure is your friend. I haven't met one successful person who hasn't echoed this sentiment—make failure a friend. I frequently apply this principle to my own life. I challenge you to research three successful people worldwide, and I guarantee you they've had more failures than successes. But they've made failure their teacher and friend instead of their enemy.

I truly get this struggle from my own personal challenges in the past. There is no way to escape this. When your inner world is conflicted and misaligned, you cannot focus on the principles required to succeed. In a sense, this will always result in mediocrity. I was literally my own biggest enemy to success for many years. When I became serious about success, this was another personal challenge I became dedicated to overcoming. This is how I know the power and impact of the principle referenced in this step: the 360-degree internal walk-around.

What I shared in Steps One through Four will serve as building blocks for what we will walk through in this next step. As we continue discussing these principles, I want to make it clear that each step will build on the next.

> You can't skip over a step that is more difficult than another and expect results. You may feel like you made some progress, but you will end up getting in your own way. Don't do yourself that disservice.

Skipping any part of the steps is equivalent to taking a test and not studying a chapter the test will cover. Your results will be average at best. I am not sharing this to discourage you. My goal is to encourage you because adequate preparation with expectations and small wins along the way will keep you moving forward. Retraining your thinking involves this understanding since thoughts shape how we view ourselves. Through it all, we can choose our attitude without the excuse of our circumstances. Building on the fact that everything works together, we can use our pictures from Step Four to start our internal walk-around. As we go further into Step Five, we'll cover how to effectively evaluate yourself using my signature 360-degree internal walk-around process of your mind and learn how to challenge negative thoughts objectively. Let's continue with the next step toward Boundaryless Success.

IT'S TIME TO GET HONEST WITH YOURSELF

> Did you know that questions are a very effective way to discover new things, break bad habits, and form new disciplines?

As I have grown over the years, I have uncovered four questions that assist me with being brutally honest with myself. I want you to read and respond sincerely to those that resonate with you.

1. When you are alone with your thoughts, how often do you genuinely have an honest moment with yourself?
2. How do you respond when you finally have a moment of self-honesty?
3. Do you justify or take ownership of the need to move in a different direction?
4. Is it a natural thing to do, or do you struggle with self-honesty?

Self-honesty is essential. Please understand I am not referring to searching for truth that points the finger at someone else.

> I am encouraging you to get honest with yourself about where you are, how you got there, and where you desire to be and then take responsibility.

I'm not saying there weren't challenging instances that put stumbling blocks in your way. I'm saying that the only person who can affect you is you. You can't change what someone else does, says, did, or will do. All you can change is *your* thinking and response to an outside environment. One hundred percent self-honesty is the only way the 360-degree internal walk-around will work for you.

> Practicing self-honesty means: no hiding, no ignoring, no overlooking, and no denying issues that are uncomfortable to address.

On that note, I will share a timeless truth: self-honesty will be organic when the pain gets bad enough.

At this point, I request you go deep, get real, and allow this process to work for you.

> Did you know that one of the top reasons people struggle with being honest with themselves is that they do not want to come to terms with their contribution to where they are today?

Let's consider this next scenario to build on that fact. If you're in a situation where you become overweight, do you make excuses instead of saying:

- I overate every time I sat down.
- I ate three times the serving that's recommended for daily nutrition.
- I ate because I was lonely.
- I ate because I was bored.
- I filled a void with food.
- I made unhealthy food choices.

Let's review this example through the lens of self-deception.

If I decide to overeat after committing to limit my daily caloric intake, I might justify that decision with thoughts like, *I've been good all week,* or *I'm going to start a diet on Monday,* or *Life's too short not to have fun.* All of these types of thoughts are a form of self-manipulation. Essentially, when you do this, you sabotage your success with dishonesty. While this is done unintentionally in most cases, it has real consequences for goal attainment.

Self-deception manipulates the mind to do everything except what you need to do for a change. You create and accept excuses as to why you cannot do something you are fully capable of.

You are giving yourself a pass to not do what you must do even though you know better. No matter the validity of the excuse, it will not serve the future you envisioned if it is born from self-deception.

All the above excuses you are projecting from outside influences are in your control. In reality, you had the opportunity to make the right choices. You didn't like the outcome of overeating, so rather than take responsibility for your choices, you projected the consequence as if it were out of your control. When we work through the steps correctly, we can easily say, "I weigh too much because I overeat." Rather than making this a self-destructive moment, I tell myself that I fell short today, but with tomorrow comes another chance and another opportunity to improve. Do you see how this works?

I must dispel a huge lie about failure that many people struggle with: *failure makes me a bad person incapable of producing success.*

This is not true.

When you process failure honestly instead of inventing excuses, you will shift your thinking toward owning your part, evaluating to extract lessons, and implementing practices for desired success.

Evaluating failure through ownership reveals that, despite the current outcome, you have seeds of greatness waiting to be cultivated.

In this example, I shifted my perspective by looking at what I am capable of, what I am doing, and what I could have done differently, and those honest answers pointed me forward. In doing so, I reminded myself that I have the skills, intellect, and ability to succeed at a higher level. I clearly saw that I made a mistake or a poor decision that got me off track. This way of thinking motivates you forward! It energizes you to try it because you recognize you can succeed in that area.

This is also an excellent example of Step Four's principles on pictures. Let's apply all that I just explained concerning the goal of eating healthy. You started strong, but you got off track for several weeks. Getting sidelined with healthy eating goals would have gotten painful at this point, causing you to get honest with yourself and do what you were always capable of achieving success.

But if you are unwilling to have an honest conversation every time you experience failure, you will never uncover the lessons and tools that you need to move forward, leaving you stuck in the unproductive cycle of excuses.

Are you willing to put these principles into practice?

Are you ready to do the hard work until you succeed?

I will bet that your answer is yes. Willingness is all you need at this point to continue forward. Now, together let's chase out those thoughts opposing your envisioned future.

CHECKING IN ON YOURSELF

Anything that will get or maintain health requires a checkup: your physical body, your vehicle, your devices, and more. Checkups are critical to maintaining health and performance.

A checkup at this stage of your journey is so important.

> Too often, people will celebrate mediocre results when they are capable of so much more.

> Somewhere inside of you, you know that you are capable of more, and you know what you are capable of versus what you've been doing.

The opportunity is moving you closer to what you were created to achieve. Let's think about this concept a little more. Suppose I embarked on a four-month weight-loss journey. I started eating better, watching my calories, exercising daily, and resisting the urge to indulge in a cheat treat. Imagine that I did so for ninety consistent days. That's a pretty significant accomplishment, right? As I enter the final month of the journey, I get off track. I cheat in my eating, blessing myself with an extra snack here and there. No big deal, right? Wrong. As a result, instead of attaining my goal of weight loss and new eating habits, I fell short of it. Yes, I might have lost a little weight and started growing a little discipline, but I know I could have had greater results had I not gotten off track. This may sound like I'm being a little hard on myself, but we cannot give ourselves a pass.

> We must push ourselves. Otherwise, we will not tap into the motivation required to experience Boundaryless Success.

So instead of celebrating mediocre results, I evaluate myself, my choices, my results, and my goals. I intentionally look for lessons to grow forward. Have you ever experienced some results while falling short of your goals because you gave yourself a pass? In the next section, I want you to recognize and overcome the behavior that hinders your goals.

I would like for you to think through a few questions at this stage:

1. Am I capable of achieving more?
2. Do I get in my own way?
3. Why do I get off track when I'm close to my goal?
4. What could I do differently?
5. What can I learn about myself?
6. After getting off track, how do I get back on track?

These six simple questions prepare your mind to own your current position in life and are the start of the 360-degree internal walk-around. In mentoring others, I have observed a pattern of why people get stuck at this stage. Many struggle with being honest with themselves about what they have done to contribute to their own failure. By feeding into this thinking, the temptation to make excuses creeps up instead of taking responsibility.

> I believe you have to get to the root of the problem in order to change the outcome.

Excuses will never allow you to get to the bottom of anything; they only promote derailments in life. Healthy self-esteem is not just about feeling good about yourself but also about retraining your brain to align with your vision and goals. This entire book is a tool to equip you to get to where you're building self-esteem and realizing that if you're not where you want to be in life, put in the effort to get there.

Mental obstacles limit more success than physical obstacles. This is true because how you view yourself is what you manifest in your life.

> If you perceive yourself as unable to succeed in an area, then you will not.

For example, if you see yourself as powerful, unstoppable, and capable, you will operate from that perception. Likewise, you will manifest from this perception if you view yourself as weak, unworthy, and incapable. Do you see how that worked? When you change your perception of yourself, you can change your results in life.

> The 360-degree internal walk-around will enable you to understand where the negative perceptions derive from and how to get beyond them to a desired point of success.

Please don't wait until there is a necessity picture that requires you to do what you have time to do right now. What could your continued procrastination cost you? Would it be worth it? Do you want to continue to roll the dice? Now, what do you plan to do as a result of your answers to these questions?

> Awareness without execution is torture.

Why? Because you know that you have what it takes to make a change, but you are unwilling to do it. Think about it. How many promises have you broken to yourself? How many goals have you abandoned? How many dreams have you not pursued? How many projects have you started and quit?

> Aha moments, vision boards, wishes, or need will not draw success within your reach—only hard, consistent work will.

Once you are aware and committed to execution, you will experience change.

Again, you have to do the work. I firmly believe that a primary reason people fail to execute is because of the effects of low self-esteem.

Getting beyond the impact of a moment or experience that changed how we view ourselves can feel impossible. You still have to go for it.

> Fear is only as real as you allow it to be. Fear only has the power to keep you where you choose to stop. You have to face it if you intend to overcome it.

The beginning of our 360-degree internal walk-around starts with self-honesty (even if it hurts). I have shared this before, but it is worth mentioning again. You must be honest about where you are today and what has contributed to getting there. By doing so, you can stop the excuses, break patterns of unsuccess, and identify how to find the way forward after failure.

Let's go back to the principles from Step Four on the different types of pictures. There must be some kind of pain point that we're trying to correct or that we're trying to accelerate, or something where we feel like we've plateaued or hit a wall or some kind of dissatisfaction. Ask yourself:

- What am I trying to accomplish?
- Where am I trying to go?
- What have I put into my mind to get there?

I believe you are worth more than a chance at success. This is why I am encouraging you to choose to intentionally get ahead with your own 360-degree internal walk-around.

It's Time to Do the Work

Until now, we have been talking about digging deep and inspecting our choices from every angle in our 360-degree internal walk-around. Now it's time to examine this evaluation and provide clear steps to walk through.

This internal walk-around will help you determine how to pull pain forward to produce the desired change.

We don't want to wait for a necessity picture. It is about discovering what stops you from executing—the mental obstacle—and coping with stress, boredom, or stagnation.

Steps to the 360-degree internal walk-around:

- Determine what went into your mind.
- Evaluate what specific decisions or actions got you to where you are today. Complete an honest evaluation of what your contribution to it was. You must discover your complacency zone, where you repeatedly decide this is not worth pushing past.
- Own your part in the results.
- Extract the lessons as they relate to your thinking.

I've added some executable steps in this step. However, this step will require considerable thought that you will then turn into applied thinking items to change what is currently driving your thought process. In previous steps, we identified the pictures in the 360-degree internal walk-around. We are revealing to ourselves what is driving our thought process and changing those thoughts to progress toward success.

As you begin this process, I encourage you to start with a personal affirmation I've told myself for years, "Today, I will start over. I will clear my mind of yesterday's mistakes. I will apply the lessons from them, and I will execute with excellence." Congratulations, you are well on your way toward Boundaryless Success! While perfection won't be achieved immediately, meaningful progress will ensue. The simplest concepts are often easy to understand but are the most difficult to do daily.

> Never forget you are in control of yourself, even when life feels out of control.

Let's rock'n roll!

STEP SIX
REDISCOVER YOUR STRENGTHS

If you do not recognize small progress, you will give up.

When you began reading this book, did you know what your strengths were? Have your thoughts about your strengths changed or stayed the same? Do you see yourself in a different light? When you did your 360-degree internal evaluation and started being honest with yourself, did it reaffirm your strengths before this book, or did it shed new light on what could be your strength if you attempted it without the fear of failure? I firmly believe the only way to learn in this world is to take everything that's happened to us and figure out what it is supposed to teach us. This is what I would describe as a process of rediscovering your strengths.

When was the last time you spent the entire day doing something, and although you were tired, you were filled with positive energy? The kind of day where you come home, and you're exhausted but still have to get on the phone and share the amazing day you had with someone. That feeling should accompany you when operating in your strength zone. At the same time, when was the last time you did something all day and came home totally zapped? That feeling is typically triggered when you spend time in an area of weakness. I will give you some key points needed to rediscover your strengths and manage your weaknesses to truly find Boundaryless Success.

You need to begin by focusing on your strengths. How do you discover your strengths? It sounds complicated, doesn't it? Think back to when you were passionate about something but later gave it up. What caused you to give up? Was it an event, circumstance, environment, laziness, or fear? What was that thing you were so passionate about? Did you give up on it for a valid reason, or is it something that you should rediscover? Answering these questions will help you learn more about what actions you must take to set yourself up for success.

I had to ask myself these questions after a life-threatening accident in 2019. One of my passions has always been flying, but an incident almost caused me to give it up forever. After working for many years, I could finally pursue my dream of becoming a pilot. I completed the classes, training, and licensing and eventually acquired a piston aircraft. Although I was fearful and nervous about aviation, I thought I would keep myself safe by being a stickler about my maintenance. We may be defying gravity, but at least I could control how well and how often maintenance was done. The plane came with a recommended maintenance manual from the Federal Aviation Administration. I religiously did more than the recommended scheduled maintenance. If the FAA recommended changing a part after a hundred hours of flight, I would change it at fifty; I thought I would keep myself safe by doing that.

On one flight, I took off at an airport and climbed to 3,000 feet before losing power. I had a unique opportunity to rediscover a strength, but I wasn't ready yet. I had about three minutes and multiple worst-case scenarios between losing power and hitting the ground to decide. Fortunately, the plane was equipped with a parachute. However, the preferred deployment of the parachute is at 3,000 feet or above. We were gliding down to the earth while multiple alarms were going off in the cockpit, and the passengers were hysterical (rightfully so). Soon we had less than two minutes until we would hit the ground. I checked the altitude and saw that we had about thirty seconds before the parachute would no longer be an option. We were at 1,300 feet when I finally deployed the parachute. It wasn't at an optimal altitude, but it was our best choice. And while that sounds like an obvious choice, remember, when you aren't in your strength zone, it can be difficult to react, and you may be paralyzed in fear. When you are well-trained in your strength zone, this doesn't happen. Operating well is a reflex when you are in an area of strength. Luckily, aviation is a strength of mine, and by deploying the parachute, we could land safely. All four of us onboard survived.

Whether or not you are in your strength zone, when something traumatic inevitably happens, your natural tendency will be to say, "I will never do that again." And I did just that for a little while. Remember, I have a twenty-four-hour rule that guides me when something out of the norm happens, whether positive or negative. I allow myself to either celebrate or commiserate for twenty-four hours only. After that, I must let it go to push onward. I'm no different from anyone else, and fear had the tightest grip after the crash. By implementing my twenty-four-hour concept, I knew that allowing the fear to control me after that mark would have made my thoughts irrational. The longer I waited to learn the lessons, the longer it would take to start again. When I'm in my strength zone, I am still susceptible to failure and allowing that to lead me to quit.

> At this point in my life I'd had enough training to understand that by allowing failure to lead, it would've been like cancer and would have slowly crept into other aspects of my life.

A couple of days passed, and I got a call. I needed to be somewhere a long distance away, and I needed to be there fast. Driving at this point didn't seem like an option to me simply because my gut was telling me to get back up in the air. So even though there was a fearful voice in my head telling me not to, I flew again. Do note that it took six to twelve months before I wasn't replaying the crash every time I flew. But I continued to remind myself that flight is safe, flight is one of my strengths, and allowing fear to stop me would narrow my ability to grow in other aspects of my life.

Let's unpack this. This was a unique example for me, but the lessons apply to us all.

If I had never flown again, what possibilities would I have limited? I would have limited my opportunities to speak, train, touch people, and share my experiences with them so they could get further faster. My plane allows me to save time and get more done quicker since I use it as a business tool.

So, I dug in and figured out what I had done in that situation that got me in a position where that aircraft failed. Why did that happen, even though I did more than the required maintenance? That's what I mean by evaluation. I evaluated the National Traffic Safety Board findings when the engine was repaired. To sum it up in generalities, I learned that the plane—a piston-based aircraft—had an older engine design. No matter what you do, because of the way it's designed, there are going to be situations and times when those engines are going to fail, which is why when you go through aircraft training, they teach you so many safety procedures and how to get the plane down safely and preserve life. Other types with turboprops and turbine engines have a much lower failure rate. So, in this situation, I didn't quit flying. Instead, I switched to a more reliable aircraft. Does that make sense to you?

I could have decided, "I'm never going to fly again." It's no different than if I try something and experience a severe injury, right? I mean, I had a brain tumor in 2012. I had a seizure, and the doctor came into the room within forty-five minutes and told me I had metastatic brain cancer and had six months to live. I could have accepted that diagnosis. Instead, I contacted as many professionals as possible for more information. I pursued and found out that my initial bleak diagnosis came from an internist who didn't really understand what he was looking at because his specialty wasn't neuroscience.

I then found an experienced neurosurgeon who told me, "Not only is it not cancer, but it is benign, and I think we can remove it." Well, he removed it, and I lost the use of my left arm because that part of the brain operates the left side of your body. He told me that to recover, I would have to retrain my arm to move. Well, what most people don't realize, and I didn't until I got into this particular situation, was that when you're a baby, you teach yourself to move. We don't remember that specific part of our life. But if you watch babies when they walk and move their arms, they'll make that movement repeatedly until they perfect it. And it's the same way when you're retraining a part of your body after an injury. I could have just accepted that situation and reminded myself that many injured people never regained movement. But I think most of that is mental because they believe things like: *My arm doesn't work. I had this terrible thing happen to me. I had a setback. Life's unfair.* I was determined to use my arm again, so I said: "What's the solution? How do I evaluate this issue? How do I come up with the solution? How do I execute daily to do something different to the best of my ability?"

I retrained my arm through repetitive motion over and over, and over and over and over. The progress was so small that when I first started, I would show people how I was tapping my finger. I could see people looking at me like, "You poor soul, you think that is success?"

But it *was* success! I couldn't raise my hand to my eye but could move my finger up and down. Then I trained the second finger, then the third finger, and then I trained the fourth finger. I knew what it was like to have an arm that worked, right? I knew what it was like to lose the use of my arm. I knew what it was like to go from being independent to being dependent to having somebody hold my arm up in the shower to bathe, to have somebody help me tie my shoe, help me button my pants, and buckle my belt. That was the pain picture. The success picture was that I knew what it was like to do all those things independently. I knew what it was like to rely on myself to do those things. In the interim was the work.

When I started tapping that finger, I would pour sweat like I had worked out for an hour. My shirt would be wet, my face would be wet, and my hair would be wet. I could have given up and said, "I'm not doing this anymore." But I continued to remind myself, like playing a tape over and over in my mind, that I knew what independence looked like, and I was determined to achieve it.

So, with that plane crash, I evaluated my experience and knew I had to get up in the air again. I think the plane crash was on a Sunday, and I was flying again by Wednesday. I did that intentionally. Also, I did that because I had no anxiety before the incident. After that, I had fear, but I flew anyway because I knew I had to keep moving forward.

I needed to evaluate the experience and extract the lesson so that whatever my contributing factor, whatever my wrong information was, whatever my lack of teaching, whatever my lack of bringing others alongside me was, I could form a new plan so that I didn't end up with the same result.

> I knew if I didn't get up there again, the last tape I'd ever play in my mind would be of failure—over, and over, and over, and over, and over, and over again.

OVERCOMING FAILURE AND REDISCOVERING YOUR STRENGTHS

1. Why would failure occur in a strength zone?
2. When failure occurs, do you recoil or press on?
3. How can you overcome failure accompanied by fear in your strength zone?

Understand that when you are rediscovering your strengths, more than likely, they will be the same strengths as before (unless you had an unrealistic view of a strength). The hiccup occurs after a traumatic or negative experience or when you are no longer growing in strength. This commonly occurs because of unevaluated failure, causing self-doubt. In my case, failure in my strength as an aviator came from a lack of knowledge. I thought I had done everything in my power maintenance-wise for that plane to stay in the air, but it didn't. Had I known the information about the plane design, I obviously wouldn't have opted to purchase one because I'm not a risk-taker in aviation. Now I fly multiple times a week in my more reliable aircraft. No one would have blamed me for never flying again, but I would have never forgiven myself for giving up something I knew I had a passion and a strength for.

You may start strong, but sometimes you get hurt. How do you bounce back? Identify the strengths you gave up on. It depends on who you are and what step of life you're in. For some people, just being rejected by a group of friends is a traumatic failure, so I think that term is really defined by who you are as a human being. I was having a conversation with somebody not too long ago. This person said I hurt his feelings. It was minuscule to me but crucial to him. So, we have to decide for ourselves how traumatic something is. An important aspect of traumatic failure is that it comes in one of two ways—either it's a low self-esteem issue or an overconfidence issue. For instance, I think I had an overconfidence issue with aviation. I remember when I was going through flight training, and they were teaching all these safety procedures. I thought it was the most ridiculous thing I'd ever heard. With all the navigation and automation, I wondered why they still taught this 1950s-style stuff. Everything that's been done up to this point was done for a specific reason, and we've got to figure that out before we decide to change it.

After that crash, I knew immediately why they had taught all those things and made us do it repetitively. If you've been trained properly when an emergency arises, you go into a professional reflex, and you just start doing what you know needs to be done.

When we took off the day of the crash, from the time we had an engine failure until we hit the ground was three minutes. Do you think we had time to pull out the manual and start trying to retrain ourselves? We had to be trained at that moment to react immediately. When you watch professional football on Sunday, and you see a player break on a ball or pick up a fumble, that's something they've trained for repeatedly because those things happen at the speed of sound. They've watched on tape and conditioned their mind until it becomes a reflex. My brain surgery was five or six hours long, but my surgeon had trained hours and hours to be able to perform it. He wasn't sitting there trying to look at a manual and figure out what he needed to do to remove my tumor. I guarantee you every surgery is different. My surgery team probably encountered issues where my surgeon had to use his professional training and judgment to make a quick evaluation or decision. The president of our country… we don't know what he's going through now, but I guarantee there are crises. Things are popping up that he has to decide on based on his last fifty years of professional work.

In my case, what occurs with me personally and professionally is a sum of the decisions I made years ago to become a student of leadership and start professionally preparing myself. I didn't know what I was preparing for, but I was doing the work.

> I've heard a saying from the sport of boxing that says when the fight starts, the training is over. Now, you have the opportunity to execute or not, and it's based on who had the best preparation.

To tie all this back to our discussion, you must evaluate those experiences. Otherwise, you're not linking the lessons to the execution.

REGROUP AND RECLAIM

So, are you ready to rediscover your strengths? What is something that stuck out to you as you read this step? Did you think back to when you gave up on something you had a passion and talent for?

Let's review:

1. What talents have you given up on?
2. Why do you think you gave up?
3. What risk did you not identify before trying the first time that caused you to freeze?
4. What is your plan to restart?
5. Do you think you can reach excellence without operating in your strength zone?

When you answer these questions, how to apply them to move forward will become clear.

> Rediscovering your strengths sounds difficult. However, most of the answers are ones that you already know. The difficult part is making yourself go forward until the reason you gave up in the first place fades away.

As we walk through this journey together, let me encourage you that the rediscovery of your strengths will pay significant dividends. Fight against apathy or feeling like it's too difficult.

> If you gave up yesterday, today is a brand-new day.

STEP SEVEN
Creating Your New Norm

Don't accept the reality that failure paints for a moment.

Now that you have read Steps One through Six and reimagined yourself… retrained your thinking, reframed your attitude, envisioned your desired changes, evaluated your internal world, and rediscovered your strengths, how do you imagine these skills fitting into your daily life? Can you see yourself using each step to find your new norm? How does that feel? Does it excite you?

You may wonder how you create a new norm. That's a fair question. If you've gotten this far, you've read and absorbed some exciting information; however, I imagine you may still be a little timid and wondering how this applies to you. During this time in my life, I didn't call what I was doing creating a new norm, but I now know that's what it was. When I got to the reimagine yourself step, I had to focus on my self-esteem and where that could take me now that I didn't allow it to constantly hold me back from doing what I knew I could. When you're creating this new norm, at first, you will have to remind yourself continually to stay on track. How did I turn my new norm into my everyday reality? I stayed relentlessly focused on everything we've discussed thus far in Steps One through Six.

Relentlessly.

Focused.

My new norm looked a bit like this: I would start with what I knew I could do every morning. I put fresh information in my mind focusing on sales and motivation. Fresh off of improving my self-esteem, I was constantly reminding myself that I was worthy, fully able to commit to myself, and would execute on success in all areas of my life. At first, I had to remind myself daily (sometimes even more often than that) of all those things because intrusive thoughts would creep into my mind causing me to question whether or not I was capable of success. As I focused on reminding myself that I was worthy every morning, sooner or later, this was no longer consciously required because I had retrained my thinking in such a way that I had confidence in knowing I could be successful. My subconscious was also on board, feeding me what I had consciously put into my brain. Besides having to retrain my thinking as it related to my self-esteem, I also had to flush out years of self-doubt as it related to my skills, talents, and ability to execute over a long time. After years of talking to myself negatively, retraining my thinking required me to reframe my attitude. See how this all works together? Both my negative self-talk and cynical thinking led me to the need to reframe my mindset. Realizing this and attempting to control my thinking and attitude made it possible for me to wake up daily and say, "Today's a great day. I know what I'm capable of, and here are the things I'm going to do."

When I envisioned my desired changes, I would evaluate what I did the day before and put that into what I would do today. With my self-esteem on the mend, I could have an honest conversation with myself about where I had fallen short the day before. Then, I could focus on those shortcomings and the opportunity to do them differently the next day. At the same time, I could look at what I had done well and improved on from the day before, and therefore continue reframing my attitude and thinking because I was getting these small wins. All of this led me to evaluate my inner world. While I knew sales was what I was operating on at that point, it required me to have real honest conversations about my goals, dreams, and aspirations and how they related to my strengths, talents, and abilities.

> You see many people follow in the footsteps of what's easy, what their parents did, or what someone else encouraged them to do rather than looking within and seeing what they're capable of.

I don't want you to think that when you evaluate your internal world, immediately you're going to understand everything—it's not like waving a magic wand. While it sounds easy on paper, creating my new norm was choppy many days. All of this collectively is something that I consciously review more often than not. Have you ever done something unfamiliar to you, like playing a game you've never played before? People tell you the rules or how to do it. Still, once you started, it felt kind of funny, so you constantly reminded yourself of how to play or asked questions about what you were supposed to be doing. If you're like me, it felt like an out-of-body experience, which is why many people give up and quit. No one enjoys feeling uncomfortable. Many people give up on creating their new norm because it isn't easy. It will feel like an out-of-body experience until you talk to yourself so much that you think my words are your own. It'll almost feel like this has been who you are from the beginning. So I encourage you to not give up while creating your new norm, even though it may initially feel uncomfortable. While all the steps are important, this one may be the most critical because it's where many people throw in the towel and return to their old ways.

It's almost like going to the gym on the first day. You come out, and you've done very well. The next day you're excited because of your success the day before, and then, on the third day, the soreness sets in. You wake up early and are tired and sore, so you want to stay home. You tell yourself, "I'll just skip this one day. I've had three successful days. What's one day off?" When you feel this way while creating a new norm, you must fight against self-doubt.

> The feeling that you must reward yourself after only a few days of success is very common. This is your subconscious mind letting self-doubt creep in because this is where the hard work truly begins.

Understand that you will have days when everything is not perfect. You're going to fail. You're going to have times where it might not actually be failure, but it'll feel like it is all the same. Stay committed, stay focused, and remember to reimagine yourself so your self-esteem will be high enough to see failure as an opportunity.

While doing my internal walk-around, I had to figure out everything that got me to where I was and understand why I would get so close to my desired outcome yet ultimately fail. In the past, every time I would have a little success, in addition to the first four steps holding me hostage (because I hadn't done them right), the lack of evaluation would immediately get me to go back and start blaming or feeling like I couldn't, that I wasn't worthy, or simply that people like me could never experience those types of positive outcomes. I almost thought it was a mystical process based more on luck than anything else. While I was doing my 360-degree internal evaluation, I discovered my problem. Although I had the training, ability, talent, and contacts, I continually got in my own way because of how I viewed the world. I realized I was considering the world in such a way that I was a victim rather than realizing that, while I had made some mistakes along the way, I was able to rediscover what my strengths were. When I had failures, although, initially, I was in my strength zone, the self-esteem part made me do things like work at places that were not in my area of strength, even if I was doing a better-than-average job. Those opportunities were way beneath what I was capable of achieving. I assume that this has happened to you as well. It left me unfulfilled and hopeless with that gnawing feeling every day because I wanted to achieve so much more.

Once I rediscovered my strengths, I could place myself in a position to win so that while creating this new norm, I didn't get discouraged nearly as often as I would have had I not been experiencing the small wins. If you do Steps One through Six, create your new norm properly, and focus on it daily, you'll have small wins despite the setbacks you must expect.

> The small wins will give you the encouragement that will keep you on track when you have those days where you think, *It's time to reward myself.* Instead, you'll know that if you keep going, you're going to have a big breakthrough.

I kept going and going until that breakthrough happened for me. When I started this, I had bought into the process. It took me roughly a year to really start experiencing success, where I had lost the majority of the doubts and discouragement that crippled me in the past. I tell you that because I want to encourage you. The successes I experienced allowed me to continue to build and learn.

Now you're probably wondering what my new norm looked like daily. I started getting up every day at 4:25 a.m. I mean every single day, which I continue to do. The key takeaway from that is *every day*. You may not be a person who can operate in the morning. Many people get caught in that comparison trap of thinking, *Well, I'm not a morning person, so I can't do what he did*. If we go back to the evaluate your internal world step, we will figure out what kind of person we are and our patterns. If you do great work late at night, do those things late at night, but do them consistently and do it every single day. If it's Christmas time, I get up at 4:25 a.m. because I'm keeping the commitment that I made to myself.

If I can't keep a commitment to myself, how do I keep my commitments to others?

We all tell ourselves that we would like to exercise, read more, or have some other type of commitment, but we just don't have the time. We make time for what's important in our lives. You don't miss Christmas, you don't miss a significant birthday, and you don't miss an important work commitment.

Again, we make time for the things that are important to us.

The reason I got up that early was to read in the areas in which I was trying to grow. Every day after reading, I would exercise for a minimum of thirty minutes. I did this to relieve myself of stress and anxiety and to have general energy to have a great start to the day. I would eat a light breakfast, then shower. Afterward, I would review the plan I'd made for myself the previous day. I would get in the car no later than 6:45 because I wanted to be at my first stop by 7:30.

Obviously, many of you reading this will have different occupations and schedules. But the important lesson here is that you must be so committed that you are willing to do what others are not to achieve your goals, dreams, and aspirations. My competitors in this business would never show up anywhere first thing in the morning because they gave themselves a pass and said, "People in our industry don't want to see somebody that early." The reality was actually the opposite. They wanted to get that knocked out of their day so they could move on and succeed in the places they had to be for the day. After a full day's work, I would make my calls to set up my next day for success. Typically, at the end of the day, I would check into my hotel, handle important communications with my home office, and unpack my stuff to be ready to go to bed after dinner. I always went to bed each evening by 8:30. Again, don't focus on the times but rather the discipline, consistency, and commitment. When you make those commitments to yourself, value them just like you would a promise to your kids, your significant other, your parents, or any other important people.

What's more important to you than you?

Before I went to bed, I would make a timeline of what I would do the next day. I would review what I did that day versus what my goals were at the beginning of the day. Then, I would see what I did I wanted to do and what I didn't. The things that I didn't do were the opportunities for tomorrow. I also created a network of people inside my organization who I could call, which I did daily, and encourage them and keep myself motivated. As you start your journey, I want you to think about creating a network of people with whom you can do the same.

I'm sure many of you are probably saying, "Well, what about family time? Time for personal activities?" Again, as I stated in the previous paragraph, don't focus specifically on what I'm doing or did. Focus on the commitment to yourself. I was a traveler, so most days, I was on the road, and my schedule looked like that and worked for me at the time. Many of you will be at home, so you'll make time for family, friends, and personal stuff. I make the same commitments to myself as it relates to my personal life as I do to my professional life—but we'll get into that in later steps. The key point is to create your new norm related to Steps One through Six.

If you've gotten this far, I assume you're committed to yourself and need help to tie those steps together to create your new norm and set yourself up for Boundaryless Success.

> Think of this book as a guide to use to inspire you to reimagine yourself, to retrain your thinking, to reframe your attitude, to envision desired changes, to evaluate your internal world, and to rediscover your strengths, all of which will lead to creating your new norm.

Now with your new norm ready, let's turn the page so that you can take this with you as we develop your personal growth plan.

PRACTICAL STEPS FORWARD

1. Apply Steps One through Six. Don't move forward until you feel confident in each step.

2. Visualize your new norm. How does it feel? How will it feel when it's your reality? Now, remember those feelings daily.

3. Stay committed and on track. Measure your progress every day so that you know what to tackle tomorrow.

4. Create and schedule for yourself if you need to. We are striving each day for progress, not perfection.

5. Live out your new norm and commit to it consistently and relentlessly.

STEP EIGHT
DEVELOPING A GROWTH PLAN

The stronger your fear, the smaller your world.

Imagine getting in the car to drive to Miami from Atlanta. When you get in the car, you realize the gas gauge is missing, the speedometer doesn't work, and you can't use your phone. Where might you end up? This scenario represents how most people live their lives. Though we won't get in a car without a clear destination and the proper equipment to take us where we want to go, we cruise through life with no sense of direction or plan to accomplish our dreams.

I lived aimlessly like this for years. I just got up in the morning and went to work or did whatever I felt like that day. I thought about changing my life, yet took no action. I lived with no plan for the future. Although I knew I needed a job, I didn't have a work plan. It was 1998, and back then, jobs were posted in the classified ads in the newspaper. I simply answered an ad, knowing nothing about the company. I thought the pay and benefits were fair, so I gave it a shot.

I'm glad I did because what I heard as a recruit for this major company changed my life. I had probably listened to the information before, but it didn't resonate with me. Sitting in a hotel venue with many other recruits, a gentleman came to the stage to speak to us. He said, "You must have a personal growth plan that you look at, check, and write out." The speaker's point was to script something out so that you could refer to it later.

He talked about having a plan for our life's personal, professional, mental, physical, financial, and spiritual aspects. I went back to my hotel room that night and wrote goals for all those areas of my life in a notebook. I then wrote precisely what I wanted to accomplish in each one of those areas. Lastly, I wrote what I wanted the results to look like and my plan to get to those results.

I centered my personal growth plan around refining my sales and motivational training, as I had determined that, at this point, those two areas would yield the best results. Ultimately, I wanted to be the best. That growth plan literally changed my life. Within one year, I was the number one salesperson for the company.

All of us have goals. That goal may be changing jobs, dieting, improving relationships, or fixing our finances. But, most don't do the extra work of planning to reach these goals. For example, if you set a goal of losing weight, the first question you must answer is, "How will you lose weight?" The answer and plan must be specific, but most people are not detailed enough to create the plan, "I'm going to eat three small meals a day. I'm going to limit my calories to 1200 a day. I will make sure that I prepare my meals on Sunday or Saturday so that I bring them with me and don't get caught in a situation where I have to eat out. I will make sure that I have a plan where I can cook at work or eat warm food." But a plan cannot be executed without specifics.

Once a plan is set, how will you check to see if you're doing it right? For example, a plan would include these actions: "I'm going to get on the scale on Monday, Wednesday, and Friday to see what kind of progress I am making. I will refer to my plan weekly to monitor my progress." Why do we need to check regularly? Because with any plan, whether a diet plan, financial plan, or professional plan, people get two or three days in and start rewarding themselves. As previously discussed, rewarding yourself prematurely hinders your ability to reach your full potential.

Your growth plan should include short-term, mid-term, and long-term goals. Your beginning focus should be on the short-term goal, including regular progress checks. A short-term goal is necessary because when reaching it will remind you how success feels, which will help you deal with discouragement when you face a failure in your mid and long-term goals (which is why the visualization step from the last step is vital). Let's say you have a financial goal. Visualize your new financial state to motivate yourself to start and focus on your plan. With that in mind, take a moment and imagine what not having to worry about finances looks like. Visualize what your bank accounts look like. Visualize what your house being paid for feels like. Visualize those thoughts, feelings, and emotions. What did that look like? What did that feel like? Now, remember those thoughts and feelings when creating your personal growth plan.

Most likely, your long-term goal is too steep a gradient to climb or effectively visualize, especially if you're starting with your first personal growth plan or working toward a goal. If you can barely cover your bills or have mountains of debt, you most likely can't visualize flying a jet around the world. When you imagine where you want to go, create smaller obtainable goals in the short-term so that when you arrive, you can celebrate and be motivated to continue long-term.

> Short-term success gives you the courage, strength, wisdom, and fortitude to keep going from one target to the next.

In my experience, a plan with shorter timeframes and regular check-ins works best regarding the likelihood of accomplishment. For example, if your financial goal is to save $1,000, break down achieving that goal to saving $200 a week. Then, check your progress each week. The first Friday, you make sure that you have saved $200. Then, in the second week, you will see the $400, which motivates you to get to $600 in the third week. Then you get excited and think, *I will get to the $1,000.*

> Short-term goals are a key part of the personal growth plan because the easiest person to discourage you is always you.

You're almost guaranteed to get discouraged if you don't have short-term wins. But, when you set up short-term goals and monitor the progress regularly, you will start experiencing wins, encouraging you to keep going.

If you don't check in weekly and decide to wait thirty days, then human nature will kick in. The first week comes, and your friend invites you to a weekend away. You think, *Well, I'll spend $200 this week and save $400 next week.* Before you know it, thirty days have passed, and you have saved nothing. Then, your self-talk turns negative, and you think, *I've never been able to save, and I still can't do it.*

In all transparency, one truth about a personal growth plan is that you will experience failures on the road to achieving your goals. Rarely do people make a plan, and everything works out perfectly; you will have setbacks. Checking your progress frequently will reassure you that when setbacks happen, you will not have declined to where restarting feels impossible. Once you identify you are off track, you can reset and get back on track. My friend Zig Ziglar once said, "Yesterday ended last night; tomorrow's a brand-new day."

> To reset effectively, you have to be willing to hold yourself accountable.

At this point, are you thinking about your personal growth plan? Are you having difficulty deciding where to start? Have you done this in the past but felt as though it lacked the detail or accountability to achieve your desired result? A buddy taught me something he learned in college, which I later applied as the steps to creating a solid personal growth plan:

- **Who** must I recruit or utilize to make my goal a reality?
- **What** is the specific goal I want to accomplish? (This should be extremely specific. Example: I want to lose ten pounds in three months vs. I want to lose weight.)
- **What** is your timeline? When are your check-in points? How will you measure your progress as it relates to your timeline? (Example: I will use a scale to weigh in every other day to stay on track with my end goal.)
- **What** and where are the places required to meet your goal? (The gym? The bathroom where your scale is? The kitchen?)
- **Why** are you setting this specific goal?
- **How** will you accomplish this goal? What tools are needed? (A scale, a gym membership, a diet plan, etc.)

How did reading that make you feel? Do you feel overwhelmed? Creating a personal growth plan sounded easy at first, right? The steps always sound simple. The daily execution is the difficult part, so accountability and checking in are crucial.

For this step, I want to focus on accountability, which is the *who* part of the plan. Ask yourself, "Who else needs to be involved to make this happen?" You need accountability, and you must decide who needs to be involved to make the goal happen. Is it your spouse, parent, friend, colleague, professional, or trusted advisor? They can hold you accountable in several ways, like helping you commit so you don't keep pushing back your start date.

Many people comment, "I can't work out by myself." They're really saying, "I can't hold myself accountable to work out, so if I have a partner, then I'm letting the partner down rather than just me because the easiest person to convince that I don't need to do something today is myself." When somebody else says, "Come on, let's go," you don't want to call and let that person down.

> We judge ourselves based on our intentions; others judge us based on our actions.

Accountability in this aspect involves letting others in on your plan. I could easily say, "Well, I meant to achieve that, and you don't understand how hard I was working. I've been working fifteen-hour days, so they can't expect me to do anything more than I was doing."

Checking your progress regularly teaches us something. Maybe your naivety or something you didn't know when you started becomes apparent as you progress and will cause you to reset and change a goal, step, or something else in the plan.

You could realize during your first weekly checkup, "Oh, I didn't know about this. I need to reset it. I need to change it. I need to stretch it. I set it too low or too high. I didn't include the right people. I don't need this, but I need that, so I may have to eliminate something." Regular short-term check-ins allow you to adjust as needed, ensure you're on the right path, and have the right resources available.

Remember when I said that if you read for five years on the same subject, you'll become an expert? If you're trying to become an expert on a topic, it could be at least five years before you achieve a vision. However, check your progress every week, every month, every quarter, and every year to see the smaller goals achieved on the way to the vision.

Let's return to the financial example. You successfully saved $1,000 in the short-term, but your long-term savings goal is $10,000. Obviously, determine how long you think it will take to reach that goal based on various factors, such as your budget, the amount of money you have, the amount of overtime you work, any side jobs, promotions, and changing positions to get involved in your strength zone, etc. Next, you must develop a realistic expectation to stretch yourself from where you are thus far and what you've accomplished. After saving $1,000 in one month, maybe you could save $10,000 in eight more months. The goal may change once you reach that benchmark, but doing what it takes to achieve it doesn't stop. After eight months, you realize, "I was able to save $10,000; next time, let's see if I can do $20,000." Then you restart, setting smaller goals and regular check-ins to note your progress.

One way to track your progress is to measure the percentage of your achievement. Though you won't be perfect in everything you do, you must still look at your percentages. For example, if you're achieving 20 percent of your goal, you likely didn't commit fully. If you're reaching 100 percent of every goal you set, you probably didn't set them as stretch goals. Your percentage of achieving your goals should be somewhere around 60 percent to 70 percent.

You want to avoid several roadblocks when setting your goal. You don't want to give yourself easy, obtainable goals that won't force you to stretch and feel pressure. Many people go through the exercise of goal-setting only to make their targets highly attainable. This temporary trick lets you tell others you've achieved a goal but leaves you knowing you fell short. Even when you meet these goals, the outcome is not rewarding.

Secondly, you don't want to give yourself an unattainable goal. Some people set overwhelming goals, like losing a hundred pounds, saving a million dollars, or paying off their house in a week—then they get discouraged because the goal is too steep of a gradient from where they are currently. One challenge we have in society is that people want instant results. I call it a pill-based society because people just want to take something to resolve everything.

There's no such thing as instantaneous results, but results occur quickly when you set short-term goals because you can see and feel that progress. You will not go from entry-level to advanced overnight. A person who is barely a good employee is not ready at this point for entrepreneurship.

> You must first seek to be the best at what you're doing right now.

Once you get to that first step, you can see the second from there, then step three, etc. You simply cannot see that last step from the first step.

Third, you must be honest with yourself to move forward. I have witnessed many people with a distorted reality. Instead of looking in the mirror every day and being honest with themselves about who they are and where they are, some people project a front to their subconscious and other people that doesn't exist.

The other day, I watched a YouTube video where two guys were test-flying an airplane. One pilot shared with the other that he planned to get an aircraft. He explained how he got down to the end of the process, but the seller wouldn't let him get a final inspection. So the pilot didn't get the plane even though he wanted it, so he could stop driving four hours to get to the test site.

Surprised, his co-pilot asked, "He wouldn't let you inspect the plane? Why wouldn't he let you inspect it?" The guy responded, "I don't know; it was weird, so I haven't bought anything yet." I believe this man was projecting to the other one that he could easily own an airplane instead of being honest and admitting, "I'm not in a position in my life yet where I can get an airplane." The reality is that he could have found 50,000 other airplanes for sale. Even if this one seller wouldn't let him inspect the plane, other people selling a plane would. If he was in the market for an airplane, he would have found one to serve his needs if he didn't want to make the drive anymore. If what I suspect is true, I'm not begrudging the man because he can't afford an airplane. However, if his goal is to buy one, he must create a plan to make that happen.

> If someone wants something, they must be willing to create a personal growth plan and be brutally honest about where they are. Also, they must be willing to write goals and actions down to hold themselves accountable.

The plan helps you stay committed to your words and actions.

The steps to creating a personal growth plan are:

1. Establish clear goals in various areas of your life.
    a. Set a goal that stretches you and places some pressure on you.
    b. Be honest with yourself about whether you're ready to pursue that goal.
2. Identify the specific steps needed to accomplish your goal.
3. Monitor, measure, and evaluate your progress regularly.
4. Be accountable.
    a. Hold yourself accountable when you deviate from the plan.
    b. Get the right *who*(s) to hold you accountable.
5. Expect setbacks, failures, and disruptions to your plan.
6. Reset your plan when needed to get back on track quickly.

When I followed these steps in 1998, they set me in motion to get to where I am today. Before then, I had plenty of goals, dreams, and aspirations, but they were all in my head. As long as they stayed in my head, nothing happened. Once I wrote them down and involved other people, I made progress. I set spiritual goals, personal goals, professional goals, financial goals, and health goals. Though I haven't been successful in all areas, I've grown from being a salesperson in an entry-level sales job to being a director of business development for that company, working for other companies, and creating my own companies. Currently, I'm a leader of an organization with 400 employees.

When I started, I had nothing and couldn't see very far, so I created small achievable goals. When sitting down that night in my hotel room to write down goals over twenty years ago, I couldn't see where I am today, so I didn't write, "I want to have 400 employees; " that was too steep of a goal to achieve from where I was then. That night, my goal was to be the best salesperson. I could visualize that. I checked my progress every week. I didn't wait because I didn't want to wonder if I was progressing. Also, I didn't want discouragement to kick in. I once read in a management publication that it's better to catch somebody doing something right and acknowledge it rather than doing something wrong and reprimanding them. So, I had to see myself doing something right to motivate myself to take the next step.

If I didn't start a personal growth plan to keep me motivated back then, I wouldn't have grown. Today, my plan is built more around leadership, personal growth, and leaving a legacy. I still create goals I can check weekly. Also, I go somewhere by myself every year for two or three days to rewrite my goals. Then, I review them weekly. Today, instead of having the goals in a notebook, I have them on my phone to look at them regularly.

Experts say that it takes twenty-one days to form a new habit. Engage with your growth plan daily; before long, it will become second nature. Also, growth plans are forever, so they never stop until someone gives your eulogy.

> People who refuse to change will encounter a world that is changing around them, and they will be woefully equipped for a world that no longer exists.

Remember, if you were going to take a trip to Miami and got in the car today with no gas gauge, speedometer, or phone, you most likely would end up in a place you didn't intend to go.

In life, if you do the work necessary to create and carry out your personal growth plan, you will get yourself where you want to be.

STEP NINE
COMMIT AND PERSIST

Success concepts are very simple; the difficulty is daily follow-through.

Have you ever created a plan but failed to execute it? Have you evaluated the reason it failed? Was it a lack of steps, planning, or the inability to execute?

Making a plan is easy. The execution is difficult, because in order to achieve excellence, we must hold ourselves relentlessly accountable in our daily activities.

Let's unpack exactly how to check your progress daily.

What do you think the first step should be to hold yourself accountable daily? Once you've finished your morning routine, reread your personal growth plan before you begin your daily activities and review the steps to execute it.

What activities can you do today that will move you closer to progress?

Again, that sounds easy, doesn't it? Remember a time in the past when you thought something was so easy that you gave yourself a pass to put it off until tomorrow. I've learned that when I skip reviewing my plan, even for one day, it leads to skipping the next morning and the next until I'm much further away than before creating my plan.

As part of the review process, I look at my yesterday. I ask myself, "Where did I succeed? Where did I fail? What was mediocre? What did I learn I need to change? Do I need to make any tweaks to my plan? Who do I need to recruit to help me move my plan forward? Do I need any additional resources?" The answers to these questions are the lessons I need to apply to my daily activities to further my progress toward my goal.

Beginning your day by reviewing the previous day's progress and applying what you learned, you focus your internal voice (and thus your thoughts) in the right direction.

> When your self-talk becomes intentional, it'll move you toward your desired objectives by holding you accountable for making consistent progress on your plan.

Although you will still make mistakes and falter, your intentional inner voice will direct you toward your desired results. When we stumble or stray—as will happen—the voice will say, "You should have done this instead," allowing us to make immediate corrections before going too far.

Before we continue, is your internal voice still negative? Are you still saying, "I can't do this?" If so, remember, the first step in achieving

Boundaryless Success is repairing your self-esteem so you can keep your self-talk positive.

> When you get off track and trust me, you will, if you haven't done the work to repair your self-esteem first, you will easily stay off track.

At this point, if your internal voice is still negative, don't think that you have failed. Simply go back to Step One. It takes time to apply each of these steps to your life, and you may need to reread a stage multiple times to figure out how it applies to you.

Think about a kid riding a bike along a trail. If the child sees a rock in the path and focuses on it, they will think, *I don't want to hit that rock. I don't want to hit that rock. I don't want to hit that rock.* Then, BAM! The child hits the rock. Obviously, the rock is a small part of the entire road. If that same child focuses on the road and where they are going rather than the rock, it never comes into focus. Instead, the rock's registered only as a subconscious thought—an obstacle to avoid—and the child can keep moving toward their destination.

So, now that you have learned the importance of reviewing and evaluating your plan daily, are you ready to take action?

> Action is what you do to implement your plan! You must do the steps you created.

Every person I know, myself included, has experienced getting up in the morning with a plan. Then, somebody calls, or a spouse or child asks a question that causes you to get involved in something you didn't intend to and diverts your plan. Setbacks happen to us all. Move on and focus on the steps. You must do the steps you created, which will take intentionality and persistence in the face of setbacks.

Thirty years ago, I heard a motivational speaker say, "You're coming to see me because you want this mystical plan; you want somebody to wave a magic wand and instantly make your goals, dreams, and aspirations come true." Unfortunately, everybody is looking for a quick, easy solution.

People often think an instant remedy is going to substitute for the hard work associated with commitment and persistence.

But life does not work that way. You must decide to apply and execute the steps outlined in this book to transform your life.

As mundane and minuscule as this process is, you must constantly review and evaluate your plan to ensure you're taking action toward your growth plan. Again, the steps are extremely simple, but the execution is difficult because you must hold yourself accountable.

If you're not ready to hold yourself accountable, then put the book back on the shelf or give it to somebody else because you're not ready to forge a new path.

Many people don't achieve their goals because they refuse to do the work. Most people get a formal education or train in a trade, then get stuck working and have no end goal for progress. They have no plan of action and no vision for the future. They wake up ten, fifteen, or twenty years later and blame others for not going further in life. They didn't go further because they didn't know where they were going.

> If I don't know where I'm going in the beginning, I'm going to end up in a place I didn't intend to be.

If you go too long without checking in on your growth plan, you can still get back on track to success. You will never execute it flawlessly. Expect to stumble; it's normal. Just don't let it become detrimental to your progress. The key is that once you realize you are off track, you understand you are human and forgive yourself. This can only happen when your self-esteem is intact. It is human nature to veer off course, so understand that fighting human nature means being intentional in your thoughts rather than letting the subconscious determine your direction. Forgive yourself, know that getting off track wasn't intentional, and remind yourself that you are talented, highly qualified, and equipped with your God-given talents and abilities. Now, understand that making a wrong choice does not define you but gives you a chance for a new decision.

Think about an area of life in which you've consistently struggled. One area I have struggled with my whole life is weight. I can't count the number of times I've had to reset weight goals. Nor can I count how many times I've failed to reach weight goals, but since repairing my self-esteem, I've never told myself, "You're a terrible person because you made those choices." I never said, "I can't do it because I made those choices." Instead, I realized I hadn't had enough pain in that area because I would decide to change when the pain became significant.

Have you had any habit or circumstance up to this point in your life where the pain has outweighed the benefits of continuing down the same path? As I shared previously, there was a period in my life when I really struggled with alcoholism. I could never have just one or two drinks. Once I started drinking, it was almost impossible to stop, significantly impacting my health and personal relationships. I could not stop drinking until I realized that the pain of abusing alcohol became greater than any benefits from drinking it. When it got to that point, I decided, "That's it." The tremendous pain motivated me to begin taking steps to change. Now, not allowing myself to drink doesn't mean I didn't have a great desire to return to it because the mind always subconsciously remembers the best of times. With drinking, my mind reminded me of when it was Friday afternoon, great weather, and my friends and I were going to sit on a patio at the bar. I forgot that when I drank too much, I often got involved in something I wasn't supposed to, did something I wasn't supposed to, got sick, missed some kind of assignment, or caused some sort of legal or financial problem. My mind returns me to the best memory, so I must intentionally bring it back to where I say, "Wait a minute, Brett!" I call it *replaying that worst tape.* When I do that, I remind myself of that pain. While my subconscious mind wants to play the highlight reel, I must intentionally play that worst tape from start to finish—consequences and all.

The pain associated with that behavior has to become greater and stronger than the temporary benefits of that activity or action. In reality, there are short-term benefits to drinking, overeating, and not managing finances. Binging on food and alcohol and overspending makes you feel good. However, the feeling is short-lived, and we soon return to the same place or one worse than before.

> Action comes when the pain gets greater than the reward.

Also, you must consider whether you're not achieving anything or only having success in certain areas of your life. In my life, I've accomplished much in my strength zone, but the weight aspect is not in my strength zone. People who don't have that issue don't understand the struggle. People are saddled with different weaknesses. Just because I'm writing this book doesn't mean I'm executing everything perfectly; I'm giving outlines and principles, but I'm not perfect. I'm human like everyone else. Writing this book means I'm not giving up. I'm continuing to push boldly forward. I keep my eyes focused on the result and will continue to pick myself up no matter how many times I fall. I just make sure that failure is not intentional. When I self-sabotage, outwardly, I'm making what appears to be the right decisions, while on the inside, I'm having a conversation with myself that impedes my success. This is why intentionality with our choices is critical because we can always choose our level of consciousness.

When I changed my career and stopped drinking alcohol, the pain outweighed the reward of false freedom of not doing what I should do. I could feel the heat and pressure rise. Finally, the pain was greater than any short-term relief from not having, much less following any plan.

Again, here are the steps to devise a plan of action:

1. Review and evaluate (check in at least three times a day on your action plan)
2. Commit to holding yourself accountable
3. Take action
4. Persist

Remember, your accountability is the plan, so you must check in with yourself in the morning, at lunch, and in the afternoon to avoid getting too far off track.

If I habitually do the same things I did before I committed to these steps, then I must look at myself and say, "Am I really committed to this? Do I really want to do this?"

STEP TEN
STAY ACCOUNTABLE

It's easy to do what everyone else is doing, but the results will be ordinary. The bold and rewarded answer the voice in their head saying, "I can be different."

One of the best pieces of advice I can give to someone on this twelve-step journey is that finding a mentor is invaluable. Going somewhere you have never been without a guide is very difficult. A mentor helps you turn your vision into results by helping you figure out how to use your talents to carry out your vision. In addition, mentors help open up things in your mind that you never thought were there and will help you get to a place you have never been.

A mentor does not have to be a living person. In fact, if you are reading this book, you are being mentored by me. Imagine me sitting there with you now, giving you access to the lessons and skills I have learned. Today's world presents us with infinite resources such as books, articles, podcasts, and live and web seminars that serve as mentors in every area imaginable. The choice is yours to determine which mentorship method works best for you. If you're like me and enjoy talking to and engaging with other people, then finding a live mentor is essential. This requires researching to find a person to speak with you and investing your time and resources in your mentorship.

Have you ever sat down and thought, "How do I get a mentor?" I have been asked how and where to find a mentor many times in my life. Most people will become frustrated looking for someone available to encourage them and show them how to be successful because it's difficult to find a mentor until you've experienced some real success. I was inspired to get a mentor when I began my personal growth journey. However, I found this problematic because I didn't have much to offer someone far ahead of me. What does *ahead of me* mean? When you first start out, even though you may have tremendous potential, you do not yet have a success record that would attract someone to want to mentor you. Though everybody wants to get started with a mentor, another hesitancy is that nobody wants to seek one out because you have to ask. Most high-powered people don't want to work with beginners until they prove themselves.

John Maxwell, a former pastor and bestselling author in leadership, explains that even on a very limited budget, he put aside money to sit down with and interview pastors ahead of him. He sent many of the top pastors during that time a letter explaining he would pay them for an hour of their time. Only a few responded and were willing to meet with him. This type of creativity is necessary to locate potential mentors to speak into your life. However, there are other ways to accomplish similar results if this doesn't work for you.

I'm not saying you won't have people close to you who want to see you succeed. Of course, successful, accomplished people are willing to mentor, and some people have the opportunity to be mentored by great leaders. However, most people will not find somebody willing to speak about their life personally and meet with them regularly. The purpose of seeking a mentor is to find someone who has accomplished what you want to do and will provide wise counsel, insight, and direction.

However, finding someone who will make themselves available can be difficult, giving us an excuse not to apply the steps.

When I use the term *wise counsel,* I mean selecting accomplished leaders in the areas you want to grow in and learning from their teachings. Wise counsel speaks to your specific goal and how to reach it, not forgiving you for not executing. In essence, what makes counsel wise is the integrity of the person giving the advice and their results in a specific area you're interested in.

Let's begin by referring to your growth plan to identify areas requiring counsel. Based on your growth plan, you may have identified fifteen areas to grow; however, focus on those that pay the highest return first.

> When you find people who are accomplished in those identified areas, accept what they're telling you rather than questioning them, and apply those things to your life.

While asking questions about the mentor's material is fine, remember that you identified these people as subject-matter experts.

> As humans, we typically go back to what's comfortable for us—our subconscious thoughts have a way of questioning new information that is foreign to our norm.

The reason that we start with the highest return first is that it is what will pay the quickest dividend for the effort being put forth. When you experience success and expertise in the initial areas, you will be encouraged to add the other areas you identified.

Initially, I needed to grow in nearly every area. Obviously, I couldn't successfully grow in several areas at one time, so I started with motivation and sales because those two areas directly impacted my desired results. My first plan was extremely elementary because I didn't know what I didn't know. As I learned what I didn't know, I had to reset directives, goals, dreams, and aspirations based on what I learned. When you start your journey, you will grow mentally, and your perspective will change. You will probably need to edit or reset your original growth plan as you discover new things. If you don't need to reset your growth plan, you need to reevaluate whether your plan includes goals that will stretch and challenge you. When you reset your plan, you reset your goals so that you can act toward your desired results.

Instead of seeking a person after writing out my first growth plan, I sought wise counsel by committing myself to reading books about motivation and sales for at least an hour a day. By doing this, I learned I could get the best mentors in this country for around twenty dollars by walking into any bookstore or finding online resources. Plus, these powerful people will mentor you anytime and any place. The beauty of a book is that you can have multiple mentors available at any time. One person won't be able to cover all the areas you need to grow in daily.

Do you enjoy reading, or do you find it painful? Whether or not you like to read, achieving growth will be difficult without committing to educating yourself in your chosen areas. I've heard people say, "I don't like to read." Guess what? I never read a book—other than what was required in school—until I was twenty-eight, but I have read thousands of books since. Back then, my negative inner voice had convinced me that I couldn't comprehend information by reading.

When I started reading again, I knew nothing about motivation, sales, or leadership. I didn't even realize just how passionate I was about those areas. But, I couldn't put books down once I figured out my talents. If you give me a textbook now about something I'm not interested in, I guarantee you that I'll revert to that fifteen-year-old student who, in today's world, would be labeled with ADHD. However, I could take that same-length book about leadership, read it, and tell you all about it the next day.

I have learned that many educational systems are designed for everybody to do the same thing rather than focusing on people's strengths and interests. Our system doesn't give a person with a love for science the opportunity to master science, nor a math person the chance to focus on math. Instead, everyone must study the same subjects for the same time. What is the outcome? Mediocrity.

> When selecting who to receive wise counsel from, your mind must first be prepared to accept the information. You will need to intentionally open your mind because the information may go against everything you've heard up to this point. The conventional wisdom you've heard will be challenged.

Many people repeat what their parents do because their parents birthed them, took care of them, and probably loved them more than anybody else. So, most people don't challenge their parents' opinions, even though their parents aren't experts in every subject. Instead, they emphasize, "Well, my momma did it, or my daddy did it this way." As great as your parents may be, they are not the best at everything. No one is. If parents recognized that they're not the best at everything, they would welcome others better at advising them and their children. This issue goes back to the self-esteem step. When parents have high enough self-esteem, they're fine with others better equipped than themselves to provide their children with information or training. When a parent doesn't have high enough self-esteem, history repeats itself until the child can decide for themselves.

You must question every choice: the who, what, when, where, why, and how. For example, a young couple marries, and the husband watches his wife cooking a ham. She cuts both ends off the ham before putting it in the pot, and he asks, "Why do you cut the ends off?" His wife responds, "I don't know... that's what my mom did." Then, she calls her mom to find out why. Her mom replies, "I don't know; that is always what I saw your grandmother do. Let's call her and ask." Next, the two women get on a three-way call with the grandmother. The grandmother explains, "My pot was too small." Without wise counsel, we will repeat the cycles of our parents. Like this mother and daughter, many blindly follow a leader, whether their parents or someone else, instead of considering, "Is this the best decision? Is this the best advice? Is this the best way?"

You can also gain mentorship by studying the lives of people you admire. Consider Mother Teresa. If you want to learn to lead, reading material about Mother Teresa would be an excellent start because she was one of the best leaders in history.

> A long time ago, I learned that leadership is influence—nothing more and nothing less.

Mother Teresa had more influence than most people who have walked the face of the Earth. She was Catholic, but she appealed to everyone. Every religious organization respected Mother Teresa, though they might not have agreed with all her views. Further, though she was wise in the ways of leadership, I wouldn't follow Mother Teresa's financial advice because she had little money. You are responsible for identifying the gifts of those you're reading, studying, listening to, or learning from.

Alternatively, should you find a mentor to meet with and be involved in your life, make sure the person is moral and doesn't have ulterior motives. Since you are a high-potential person, you may have people who want to take advantage of you or won't have your best interests at heart. These people are quickly and easily spotted because they make things entirely about themselves. Somebody trying to use you will string you along by feeding your ego, and you're most vulnerable when you don't stay humble.

> Humility keeps you from becoming enamored with yourself.

Once you think you're the best thing since sliced bread, you put yourself in a position to fail.

> Celebrate that you have unique strengths, talents, and God-given abilities, but recognize that everyone else has theirs too.

Once you start with a mentor, like I said earlier, don't get defensive when they tell you something you don't want to hear. Don't fight or resist the person, which is human nature. When someone tells me something I don't want to hear, I still have to work to not immediately lash out. I've learned to control this weakness over the years, so I don't immediately say what I think. As I mentioned in Step Six, I've learned to wait twenty-four hours. When I do, I realize the person is right 99 percent of the time. When you have an area that needs improvement, it's usually not the first time you've heard it.

> When several people say the same thing about you, it's you, not them.

If you can't fix that area, you must find somebody to help you manage the issue.

Further, when growing, you will occasionally outgrow another person's counsel. You will have received all they had to give, applied it, and be ready for a new goal or level. I no longer read books by specific authors because I've learned and applied everything they could teach me. When that happens, it's an indication that I've grown past where I was when I started reading their material and need to seek other authors who can offer me more information.

In some areas, you may have more potential than your counsel, but you should not be ahead of the person regarding results. Plenty of books are available, but some you'll discover are mundane or mediocre once you start reading them, so you must move on quickly. I've had the experience of purchasing a book and, within ten pages, thought, "This is not teaching me anything that I don't already know; maybe I should try a different author."

> Be selective in your search for counsel so that you are always engaged in the text and keep the lessons fresh and relevant. As you get exposed to wise counsel, you should experience some results or food for thought from what is being shared.

Executing your growth plan will be difficult. Commit fully. You must decide to spend time doing things you'd rather not do, such as reading, listening, and interviewing leaders who might mentor you. Pushing yourself past your comfort zone is necessary to reach certain goals. The effort required to grow is challenging. Some people will declare they're ready to grow yet explain that they haven't started because they can't find the right mentor. They may blame others or point to outside circumstances preventing them from starting. These people really mean: "I've given up; I am not serious." Don't be one of those people.

> A person truly sincere about growing will find a way.

If you find a live mentor, take advantage of your time and use it wisely. The worst thing to do is waste someone's time. You should prepare your questions and issues to be focused and ready when you sit down with your mentor. Realize that if a successful person gives you their time, they expect you to have done some work. Come focused and prepared. Don't simply ask, "Okay, so what do I need to know?" Make sure you have questions already generated. Usually, I ask people ahead of me who they are reading. I lead with the questions like, "Who are you reading? What are they teaching you? What specific lessons were you trying to garner from those people? What is their background?"

Once you find the right counsel, you ensure that you're adding accountability. You can get all the proper counsel and read the best books in the world, but if you don't hold yourself accountable and incorporate the new information into your action plan as part of your growth, it will be nothing more than wasted time. Instead, you recognize that you've learned something you didn't know before and decide what to do with that information. Do you need to tweak your goals? How can you add that information to your growth plan? How will you evaluate whether you did something with the new information? Clearly, accountability ensures that you put wise counsel in your growth plan. The benefit of having a physical mentor is that they can ask you about your results and execution. Accountability means reviewing your growth plan and taking action. Without a live mentor, your commitment to grow and learn is governed by self-accountability enforced when you realize, "I didn't do what I had planned." You take action and do better at meeting your commitment to your plan and yourself.

<blockquote>
That gnawing in your gut is the exact accountability that you seek telling you not to let tomorrow look like today.
</blockquote>

To review, here are the steps to obtaining wise counsel and staying accountable:

1. Prepare and open your mind to receive information. Be intentional and refuse to let the subconscious mind guide you.
2. Define your strengths, your abilities, where you are today, and where you want to go to determine your areas of improvement that need guidance. Identify what area(s) you want to focus on growing, starting with your strengths.

3. Get the right counsel by seeking experts, following them, and reading their materials.

4. Read and apply what you learn by putting it into your daily growth plan and evaluating it. Be open to changing the plan as you learn new concepts, ideas, and ways of doing things.

STEP ELEVEN

EXECUTE WITH EXCELLENCE

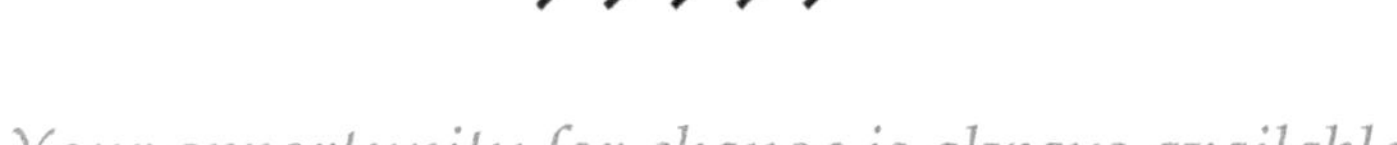

—————/////———————

Your opportunity for change is always available.
To wait for change is to delay the possible.

Now that you've reached Step Eleven, it is time to implement your plan. Are you the type of person that dives right in and gets going? Or do you sit there contemplating your necessary materials, tools, and resources rather than getting started? In a previous career, I called this *getting ready to get ready*, meaning you spend more time thinking about and planning what you want to achieve than actually getting started. Many people are excited to set goals for a new year, only to give up shortly after the year begins. They set goals, whether losing weight, improving relationships, positivity, and happiness, improving their financial position, changing careers, etc. After declaring their intent, they add, "But I'm not going to do it right now. I will start in February after I get the Christmas decorations down, the kids are back in school, and I pay the Christmas bills. After I do all those things, I will definitely start."

The new year starts, and before you know it, February arrives. The person excited about making changes in the new year has to explain why they haven't started pursuing those goals, "January has already passed. A couple of things came up that I didn't expect. Since it's already mid-February, I'll get started on April 1. After the first quarter, I will get ready to do this."

Giving themselves two more months to get ready, the person realizes that April 1 comes quicker than planned. The person explains why they still aren't prepared to start. The person needs to talk to a few more people, fine-tune the plan, visit a gym, and meet with a financial analyst. The person declares, "I have almost everything I need, so I'll start mid-month."

You can see the pattern forming. Mid-April arrives, and the person has more reasons to delay, "It's almost Easter, and I can't really do anything around Easter. I can't start this financial plan because I will blow the budget. I need to get Easter baskets and clothes for church, plus we're going on vacation for spring break. Also, a few things came up that I didn't know about at the beginning of the year, so I'll wait until May."

A month into the second quarter, the person still isn't ready to start: "The kids are almost out of school, and I had to take two extra trips for work. Plus, I became busier than I was supposed to be. I'm going to wait until June." You guessed it! June comes with no plans to start on the goals set in December. The person justifies postponing some more, "You know, I've already waited through April and May, so I'm going to wait until the summer is almost over. I'll start in August."

Yet, August brings another reason to delay getting started. "The kids are returning to school, and I have so many other things to do. I just can't do it now. So, I'll start in September; that is the best time to do it anyway. It will be fall, so the weather will start cooling off. When the better weather comes, I'll get started."

In September, they rationalized, "Fall activities started, and I was so busy that I never got started. October, for sure."

Finally, it's October, but they remember that "Halloween is coming up. My parents said they were coming to see me. A couple of things popped up at work, so November will be the best time."

Of course, when November arrives, so does the holiday season, and they say, "Nobody starts anything in November or December. I'll start fresh on January 1."

Did you catch yourself saying, "This is me?" Most people get ready to get ready in every area of life. They prepare to start because, as I shared in an earlier step, people judge themselves based on their intentions, while others regard them based on their actions.

> Knowing what they intended to do, people will give themselves a pass.

People don't hold themselves accountable because they refuse to be self-aware.

> Sincerity comes from not procrastinating and immediately taking action. Execution separates the sincere from the insincere—the doers from the talkers.

Which do you want to be? Unfortunately, there are more talkers than doers—which one are you? When a person takes steps to achieve goals, the obstacles still exist: the kids are still going back to school, the unexpected will still pop up, and seemingly impossible situations will still occur. However, successful people are the ones who take action to figure out how to maneuver any obstacle. Working through setbacks truly sets the doers apart from the talkers. When a person is sincere, it doesn't matter what problem comes up today, tomorrow, next week, or the week after—that person takes action.

While writing this book, I had several missteps, most of which were self-inflicted. Once I experienced the setbacks, I could have said, "Well, I knew I couldn't write a book." I guarantee you would not be reading these words if I still suffered from low self-esteem. Instead, I responded to the obstacles in another way; I said, "Okay, maybe I was overzealous in my first projection. Maybe, I wasn't as sincere as I needed to be to get to the finish line. So, I'm going to reset the goalpost, keep moving forward, and get to the end result."

My personal tagline is *Execute With Excellence.*

To me, to execute is simply to take some type of action. When I execute, I work daily to move some of my agenda forward: personally, professionally, spiritually, financially, and physically. In daily life, execution is intentional for each area of my life. Excellence doesn't mean I do everything perfectly or flawlessly, but I always keep moving forward. Some people write to me on social media about their interpretation of what I say about excellence. Though they make jokes, I don't take their comments personally because those people truly can't look at themselves sincerely and admit, "I didn't execute." People comment like, "Nobody can do it," because they are unwilling to follow the steps and hold themselves accountable.

When a person does accomplish their plan, it reveals the efforts that the naysayer was not willing to make.

> The truth is that we are all perfectly capable and wired for greatness. But, if we lose belief in ourselves, we allow our environment to influence us into thinking we are wired for mediocrity instead.

When I fail to execute, rather than beating myself up, I focus on what actions I took or did not take that led to the failure. Only then can I learn from my mistakes and prevent myself from making them again. Often, I find that self-doubt, worry, fear, anger, and procrastination led to my lack of execution. I have faced these negative emotions and have had to grow beyond those self-defeating limitations.

I continually refer to the story of making my first sale because it was such a critical point in the turnaround of my life. I was scared to sell because I had low self-confidence when I started my career. My upbringing was healthy and normal, and I think I had a fairly happy childhood. My parents never tried to discourage me by saying things like "You can't." However, my self-confidence was very low because of self-doubt and a weight issue contributing to low self-esteem. Whether or not we admit it, many of us have areas where self-doubt lowers self-esteem.

> Most people's self-esteem is driven by the comparison trap. They compare themselves to others rather than being driven by their own talents and developing those talents into skills leading them to execute with excellence.

In my younger years, I did what many adolescents do: I tried to be like everyone else. The problem was that I had no clue what my talents were, and I was drawn to behaviors that made me mediocre by following the crowd. Can you think of things you have done similarly that may lead to mediocrity?

Instead of exploring my interests, I tried to play team sports. My parents didn't force me to play any sport; I forced it on myself because I didn't have enough discernment to know I wasn't good at athletics. Today, I can openly admit that I'm not a good athlete, but as a middle and high schooler, I didn't accept that reality even though, in my gut, I knew that to be true. As a fifteen-year-old boy, I wasn't equipped with enough wisdom to realize that I wasn't operating in my strength zone and setting myself up for success.

To build self-esteem, you must focus on your strength zone; however, you must start by experiencing small wins before those can develop into big wins. As an adolescent, not feeling like I fit in, not connecting with others, and trying to be something I wasn't put me in a position to experience many failures. I continually wasn't winning. Had I positioned myself to accomplish this by pursuing my interests, I would have experienced success much earlier in life.

Let this experience be a lesson for parents reading this book: focus on your children's strengths and help your child focus on what they do well. Not every kid needs to participate in every activity. Let a child focus on what they are drawn to and have an aptitude for. If you, as the parent, didn't do an activity or interest, be excited for your children rather than forcing them to be what you want them to be or to fit in with their peers.

> Some people think maturity comes with age, but sometimes, age comes alone.

Many people in their thirties, forties, and fifties still try to fit in and do what is popular because that's what they have always done.

As a result of having such low self-esteem, I was saddled with the belief that I couldn't take action. In my gut, I thought I had the answers. I always felt like I could do more but was scared to act because of self-doubt, worry, and fear. When I became an adult with responsibilities, I still wasn't executing until my pain finally became greater than the benefit of sitting still. I had to find a way forward.

At this point, I had quit several sales jobs. Though I had the proper training and was well-equipped, I was still fearful and full of the doubt and anger accompanying low self-esteem. One day, I decided to try to sell something because I didn't know what to do if I had to quit another job. So, I tried even though I was terrified. After several attempts, I made a sale. I mentioned earlier that this was the first small win that changed the voice in my head from *I can't* to *I can*. This was the day I learned you must always execute even if it makes you uncomfortable. I went into detail about my life before my success because I was already equipped with the skills to succeed, but my mindset was holding me back. When you begin your journey to success, you may need training in an area to accompany and assist your mental change. If you execute without the skill set, you'll affirm the negative voice that says *I can't* simply because you haven't prepared properly.

> A great lesson I discovered from this experience can help anyone dealing with fear: you should do the things you're most fearful of because you will find that most of the scenarios you create in your head don't come true.

When I went out and pitched a sale that day, the woman I spoke to said yes, which boosted my confidence. I thought, *Wait a minute, I can do this.* What I had imagined was that I would face rejection, but my experience proved me wrong. I had conjured so many negative scenarios, yet none of them happened. So again, execute anyway, no matter how fearful you are.

Earlier in the book, I shared that everything you *think* is a reality almost always turns out to be the opposite. In sales, I learned that most people think the best salespeople are extroverted, social, gregarious people who get along with everybody. In reality, those types are the less successful salespeople. Because they're people pleasers doing what they can to please others rather than finding satisfaction from within.

> I realized that it's possible to execute through your fears, but I'm not sure if it's possible to execute through your weaknesses.

Sales was not an actual weakness of mine; it was a *perceived* weakness. In previous steps, I explained the importance of determining strengths and weaknesses. Do a deep, internal evaluation to decide what you think might be a weakness and then determine if this weakness is actual or perceived.

> When you have an area that you need to execute in that is not a strength, it will be possible when you bring someone alongside you that is strong in your area of weakness—but you must still recognize your limitations and what success looks like for you in that area.

The reality is that I am still weak despite my best efforts regarding my weight. I'm never going to have a "perfect" body because I don't have the genetics, but that doesn't mean I can't try to be healthy.

Because I had a weight problem as an adolescent, I always wanted to be physically fit and athletic. So I hired a trainer to teach me what works best for my body type and hold me accountable. Since then, I have accepted that I don't need a chiseled body; I simply need to fuel my body with the right foods and stay healthy. Without my trainer as my accountability partner, I would have never consistently executed my fitness plan.

Coaching and mentorship in a strength area or talent zone differ significantly from bringing somebody alongside you to compensate for your weaknesses. In areas of weakness, you must solicit the support you need to enable execution and achieve your desired success. In areas of weakness, you often need somebody to drag you just to be mediocre. For instance, if you're weak in finances, you want to find a counselor to help you manage your budget, and you must execute the individual expenditures. The realization is that you'll still be weak in finances, but with continual support, you can improve.

The ten steps that preceded this one help you get started. You can have the best-laid plan, but it's nothing more than a useless piece of paper if you don't execute it. It is your responsibility to complete the steps.

If you made it to this step, you have execution inside you. The people incapable of executing won't get past Step One. When they try to fix their self-esteem, they will respond with, "I can't do this; woe is me," and have a pity party.

Too often, people want instant gratification or instant results. Like those old science-fiction movies, they want to put a few chemicals in a bottle, shake it up, drink the potion, and have it magically fix everything for them.

There are no quick fixes. You must take actions that move your agenda forward in all areas of your life every hour, every minute, and every second. That is the secret formula.

You must execute. Don't be the person who is always getting ready to get ready.

STEP TWELVE
REEVALUATE, REVISE, CONTINUE

Success is not defined by money—success is defined by accomplishments.

If you made it to this final step, I believe you have put a plan together, followed the steps, and may be taking action to execute it. The person you were when you began this journey is evolving. Seeing changes in yourself will drive you to want to reevaluate, revise, and continue forward with your plan. Your fundamentals and the person you are within have not changed, but if you're growing, your thoughts and ideas differ from when you started taking action. Your mindset is changing because you've learned new information that helps you make new decisions. Therefore, reevaluation is essential if you are sincere about your growth journey.

As I've shared throughout this book, I wanted to be the best salesperson I could be when I started my personal growth journey. I had no vision to be a motivational speaker or author. I had no idea about having my own businesses or developing real estate. At that point, I could only see myself being the best corporate employee I could be. At that time, I saw myself as a senior director, staying at that company my entire career. As I continued my personal growth journey, I started looking within and recognizing my strengths, talents, and abilities.

These realizations changed what I wanted to be and do, so I had to rewrite my personal growth plan and pursue a different path.

I went from sales and motivation to a focus on leadership. In fact, I read leadership materials for probably eight years before I became a leader. I can recall sitting in my room reading a book on leadership and thinking, "I'm reading this, but I don't even lead people."

> A key point I've learned is that you may not use information today, but you must visualize where you're going because what you do today will set you up for what you're going to do tomorrow.

If you stop progressing on the steps today, what are you setting yourself up for tomorrow? There's no such thing as, "I have arrived, and I can stop." You're either expanding or contracting; there's no treading water in life. If you stop growing today, then the result of that will manifest one, three, or maybe five years from now. We can all point to examples of people who operated at a high level but stopped growing. We can think about musical artists, athletes, doctors, or lawyers who had success and then lost it. When you stop growing, you stop succeeding.

> Realize that the effort you put forth today to reevaluate and revise will move you forward tomorrow. Evaluation is your motivation to continue to review and change your growth plan.

Ask yourself daily, "What have I done today that will contribute to where I want to be in five years?"

When I birthed the idea of writing a book, the content and the vision I had in mind were much different than they are today. As the concept developed, I thought the book would be more in line with what I had read from other authors. As I kept growing and reevaluating, I decided to write about something unconventional compared to the books by those authors. Still, my vision remained the same: try to reveal individuals to themselves and get them to go further faster by borrowing from my experiences and lessons I had learned the hard way.

This leads to a key point: many people mistakenly say, "Well, I can't learn anything from anybody; I must learn the hard way." The truth is there's not enough time in this life to learn things the hard way. Get where you want to go faster by learning from others. As stated in a previous step, true wisdom comes from picking wise counsel and being selective of the kind of people you follow. You must make sure those people align with your core values because you will take their mistakes and lessons and apply those principles to your life.

The reevaluation process involves constantly looking at the plan and seeing how you are growing.

Daily, I examine and reexamine my plans and ask myself: "Are the long-term visions, plans, and goals still accurate for what I'm doing?" Whenever I confidently answer yes, I share them with others to hold myself accountable. For example, all the key leadership teams in my business know the goals I have for the company. Sharing these goals with them pushes me to hold myself accountable to plans and execute them. Also, sharing this information with my employees teaches them the importance of setting goals and seeing them through.

In addition to helping me not to get too comfortable, sharing these goals with them gives them hope for their futures.

> Though many people define success by wealth, I define success as what you are capable of doing versus what you are doing.

When you finish this life journey, what you will regret on your deathbed are the things you didn't accomplish that you knew you could have.

As you reevaluate, you must fight against that natural tendency to repeat old habits. Growth takes you out of your comfort zone; it requires you to do things you haven't done. Growth demands you to stretch beyond the realm of your recurrent patterns, themes, and thoughts. Though you will continue to do things within your talent zone, you will also do things differently than ever before.

When you reevaluate, you may think, "That isn't generating the results that I really thought; maybe I should let that go." In those moments, you need to be completely honest with yourself and ask, "Do I want to stop because it's too hard or because it's really not something I should be focused on?"

> When you start accomplishing your goals, you will be eager to reevaluate because it's not self-defeating to rework the plan when you know you are executing.

It will be interesting to see how your thought process changes from the beginning, and you will be motivated to reevaluate, revise, and move forward. You will want to share your progress with your spouse or partner, children, and others important to you.

When you're not progressing, you will procrastinate and will want to delay reevaluation because deep down, you will already know the answers, but you kicked the can down the road so that you could delay reality today.

People typically procrastinate when they don't do the work. So, you must pull that mirror back in front and ask yourself, "What did I do today? What am I capable of? What did I not execute?" The answers give you the chance and motivation to act tomorrow.

Most people don't push themselves to be excellent. I remember someone calling to share their struggles with me. The person said, "I just feel terrible. I don't feel like I'm going in the direction I want." So, we started reviewing this person's goals; then, I started breaking down what the person needed to do to get there. We quickly realized that it was the basics that the person was missing. My friend already knew what to do, but he wasn't willing to do the work required to win.

If I had the opportunity to sit down with you right now and you could share some areas you're struggling in, I guarantee you would already know many of the answers; you just aren't executing the solutions. You're not implementing them because the pain hasn't gotten bad enough to drive you to want to make a change.

The right questions to ask yourself when reevaluating are:

1. Does this initiative I've set forward align with where I am today?
2. What have I learned today that I didn't know when I started that is changing the outcome of where I'm going?
3. What new plans must I incorporate to get me where I want to go?
4. What do I need to take out based on what I've learned, not based on what I want to give up on?
5. Am I being 100 percent honest with myself daily?
6. When reviewing and evaluating, am I writing down situations and assessing information to hold myself accountable, or am I giving myself a pass because I'm not pushing myself to be excellent?

These questions will lead you to the same thing every time: make a plan, including detailed action to accomplish the plan, take action, and evaluate the plan.

In closing, I want to remind you that I grew up an average person who felt I had more to offer this world. I'm not telling you that I'm making any huge impact now, but I'm executing at a higher level than I was when I started. I always knew I had more to offer than what I was accomplishing. When I heard that gentleman give me some practical steps at that sales conference more than twenty years ago, it sparked me to embark on a personal growth journey. Many years have passed since then, and much has changed, but the 12 steps remain the same. They are a product of the many lessons I've learned on my journey (one I'm still on). I pray they touch and impact you as much as they have affected me.

As I follow the steps I've laid out in these pages and continue to evaluate my growth plan, I have developed a passion for people on this everyday journey with me, hopefully, you. I see many people who follow various processes they think will make them successful. They think getting a degree, applying to a particular company, or buying a specific house will magically start them down the path to where they want to be. For example, I've spoken with people who want more education, but that education has nothing to do with where they're trying to go. Still, they tell me, "I just think that it would be good to be educated in that subject." In pursuing that education, they take time out of the initiatives that could move them forward just to say that they earned a specific certificate or degree. Instead, they could educate themselves in the areas that will advance them toward their goals. Much of the time, that type of knowledge doesn't require formal education.

> The reality is that you must take the time to figure out what you're working for daily.

You should write down your goals, dreams, and aspirations and their results. You must identify your talent set, what motivates you, and where your strength zone lies. Once you do those things and follow a plan, your vision for health, wealth, and happiness will become clear.

Shorten your road to success by applying the *12 Steps of Boundaryless Success* in your life. Remember, success is not defined by money. Success is defined by accomplishments and can range from aiming to be the best mother or father you can be, to making one sale, to owning your own company. If success is your goal, apply these principles to do just that.

> You must be intentional and follow a plan. I am sharing the information that I had to get the hard way, so that you can begin to experience success now.

I suggest you continue to study this book until you can repeat the words and concepts as if they were your own.

That's when you know that they are a part of your subconscious and conscious thoughts and you will truly be executing with excellence.

CONCLUSION

Since you picked up a copy of *The 12 Steps to Boundaryless Success*, obviously, you want to change something in your life or discover something that will get you further faster. In this book, I've laid out personalized steps designed for you to follow that are unique to your situation.

Now that you have completed the book, you probably think, "I've got this!"

My hope for you is that you do have this. However, to make this a part of your life, you're going to have to read it, reread it, read it again, get the audio version, listen to it, and then speak it as much as possible until you hear yourself saying the words and don't even realize where they came from. Doing this will become part of what I call your 'professional reflex,' meaning you've retrained yourself in thinking, acting, and executing.

I pray that you're ready for this journey, that this book has opened pathways in your mind, and that you know what's possible. However, it's up to you to act. You can reach us on Facebook, Instagram, Twitter, and LinkedIn or on the website at WWW.BRETTOUBRE.COM. Feel free to contact us anytime. We will reply and do whatever we can to serve you. Thank you so much for your investment in us; trust me, we are invested in you.

BRETT K. OUBRE

6074 Highway 84 East

Ferriday, LA 71334

504-800-6088

customercare@brettoubre.com

www.ingramcontent.com/pod-product-compliance
Lightning Source LLC
Chambersburg PA
CBHW070818160726
48004CB00001B/320